MASTER THE™ DSST®

Introduction to Business Exam

About Peterson's

Peterson's® has been your trusted educational publisher for more than 50 years. It's a milestone we're quite proud of, as we continue to offer the most accurate, dependable, high-quality educational content in the field, providing you with everything you need to succeed. No matter where you are on your academic or professional path, you can rely on Peterson's for its books, online information, expert test-prep tools, the most up-to-date education exploration data, and the highest quality career success resources—everything you need to achieve your education goals. For our complete line of products, visit www.petersons.com.

For more information, contact Peterson's, 4380 S. Syracuse Street, Suite 200, Denver CO 80237; 800-338-3282 Ext. 54229; or visit us online at **www.petersons.com**.

ISBN: 978-0-7689-4457-0

Printed in the United States of America

10 9 8 7 6 5 4 3 2 1   24 23 22

Contents

Contents

Before You Begin

HOW THIS BOOK IS ORGANIZED

Peterson's *Master the*™ *DSST® Introduction to Business Exam* provides a diagnostic test, subject-matter review, and a post-test.

- **Diagnostic Test**—Twenty multiple-choice questions, followed by an answer key with detailed answer explanations
- **Assessment Grid**—A chart designed to help you identify areas that you need to focus on based on your test results
- **Subject-Matter Review**—General overview of the exam subject, followed by a review of the relevant topics and terminology covered on the exam
- **Post-test**—Sixty multiple-choice questions, followed by an answer key and detailed answer explanations

The purpose of the diagnostic test is to help you figure out what you know—or don't know. The twenty multiple-choice questions are similar to the ones found on the DSST exam, and they should provide you with a good idea of what to expect. Once you take the diagnostic test, check your answers to see how you did. Included with each correct answer is a brief explanation regarding why a specific answer is correct, and in many cases, why other options are incorrect. Use the assessment grid to identify the questions you miss so that you can spend more time reviewing that information later. As with any exam, knowing your weak spots greatly improves your chances of success.

Following the diagnostic test is a subject-matter review. The review summarizes the various topics covered on the DSST exam. Key terms are defined; important concepts are explained; and when appropriate, examples are provided. As you read the review, some of the information may seem familiar while other information may seem foreign. Again, take note of the unfamiliar because that will most likely cause you problems on the actual exam.

After studying the subject-matter review, you should be ready for the post-test. The post-test contains sixty multiple-choice items, and it will serve as a dry run for the real DSST exam. There are complete answer explanations at the end of the test.

OTHER DSST® PRODUCTS BY PETERSON'S

Books, flashcards, practice tests, and videos available online at www.petersons.com/testprep/dsst

- A History of the Vietnam War
- Art of the Western World
- Astronomy
- Business Mathematics
- Business Ethics and Society
- Civil War and Reconstruction
- Computing and Information Technology
- Criminal Justice
- Environmental Science
- Ethics in America
- Ethics in Technology
- Foundations of Education
- Fundamentals of College Algebra
- Fundamentals of Counseling
- Fundamentals of Cybersecurity
- General Anthropology
- Health and Human Development
- History of the Soviet Union
- Human Resource Management
- Introduction to Business
- Introduction to Geography
- Introduction to Geology
- Introduction to Law Enforcement
- Introduction to World Religions
- Lifespan Developmental Psychology
- Math for Liberal Arts
- Management Information Systems
- Money and Banking
- Organizational Behavior
- Personal Finance
- Principles of Advanced English Composition
- Principles of Finance
- Principles of Public Speaking
- Principles of Statistics
- Principles of Supervision
- Substance Abuse
- Technical Writing

Like what you see? Get unlimited access to Peterson's full catalog of DSST practice tests, instructional videos, flashcards, and more at **www.petersons.com/testprep/dsst**.

Chapter 1

All About the DSST® Exam

WHAT IS DSST®?

Previously known as the DANTES Subject Standardized Tests, the DSST program provides the opportunity for individuals to earn college credit for what they have learned outside of the traditional classroom. Accepted or administered at more than 1,500 colleges and universities nationwide and approved by the American Council on Education (ACE), the DSST program enables individuals to use the knowledge they have acquired outside the classroom to accomplish their educational and professional goals.

WHY TAKE A DSST® EXAM?

DSST exams offer a way for you to save both time and money in your quest for a college education. Why enroll in a college course in a subject you already understand? For more than 30 years, the DSST program has offered the perfect solution for individuals who are knowledgeable in a specific subject and want to save both time and money. A passing score on a DSST exam provides physical evidence to universities of proficiency in a specific subject. More than 1,500 accredited and respected colleges and universities across the nation award undergraduate credit for passing scores on DSST exams. With the DSST program, individuals can shave months off the time it takes to earn a degree.

The DSST program offers numerous advantages for individuals in all stages of their educational development:

- Adult learners
- College students
- Military personnel

Adult learners desiring college degrees face unique circumstances—demanding work schedules, family responsibilities, and tight budgets. Yet adult learners also have years of valuable work experience that can frequently be applied toward a degree through the DSST program. For example, adult learners with on-the-job experience in business and management might be able to skip the Business 101 courses if they earn passing marks on DSST exams such as Introduction to Business and Principles of Supervision.

Adult learners can put their prior learning into action and move forward with more advanced course work. Adults who have never enrolled in a college course may feel a little uncertain about their abilities. If this describes your situation, then sign up for a DSST exam and see how you do. A passing score may be the boost you need to realize your dream of earning a degree. With family and work commitments, adult learners often feel they lack the time to attend college. The DSST program provides adult learners with the unique opportunity to work toward college degrees without the time constraints of semester-long course work. DSST exams take two hours or less to complete. In one weekend, you could earn credit for multiple college courses.

The DSST exams also benefit students who are already enrolled in a college or university. With college tuition costs on the rise, most students face financial challenges. The fee for each DSST exam starts at $100 (plus administration fees charged by some testing facilities)—significantly less than the $750 average cost of a 3-hour college class. Maximize tuition assistance by taking DSST exams for introductory or mandatory course work. Once you earn a passing score on a DSST exam, you are free to move on to higher-level course work in that subject matter, take desired electives, or focus on courses in a chosen major.

Not only do college students and adult learners profit from DSST exams, but military personnel reap the benefits as well. If you are a member of the armed services at home or abroad, you can initiate your post-military career by taking DSST exams in areas with which you have experience. Military personnel can gain credit anywhere in the world, thanks to the fact that almost all of the tests are available through the internet at designated testing locations. DSST testing facilities are located at more than 500 military installations, so service members on active duty can get a jump-start on a post-military career with the DSST program. As an additional incentive, DANTES (Defense Activity for Non-Traditional Education Support) provides funding for DSST test fees for eligible members of the military.

More than 30 subject-matter tests are available in the fields of Business, Humanities, Math, Physical Science, Social Sciences, and Technology.

Available DSST® Exams

Business	Social Sciences
Business Ethics and Society	A History of the Vietnam War
Business Mathematics	Art of the Western World
Computing and Information Technology	Criminal Justice
Human Resource Management	Foundations of Education
Introduction to Business	Fundamentals of Counseling
Management Information Systems	General Anthropology
Money and Banking	History of the Soviet Union
Organizational Behavior	Introduction to Geography
Personal Finance	Introduction to Law Enforcement
Principles of Finance	Lifespan Developmental Psychology
Principles of Supervision	Substance Abuse
	The Civil War and Reconstruction
Humanities	**Physical Sciences**
Ethics in America	Astronomy
Introduction to World Religions	Environment Science
Principles of Advanced English Composition	Health and Human Development
Principles of Public Speaking	Introduction to Geology
Math	**Technology**
Fundamentals of College Algebra	Ethics in Technology
Math for Liberal Arts	Fundamentals of Cybersecurity
Principles of Statistics	Technical Writing

As you can see from the table, the DSST program covers a wide variety of subjects. However, it is important to ask two questions before registering for a DSST exam.

1. Which universities or colleges award credit for passing DSST exams?
2. Which DSST exams are the most relevant to my desired degree and my experience?

Knowing which universities offer DSST credit is important. In all likelihood, a college in your area awards credit for DSST exams, but find out before taking an exam by contacting the university directly. Then review the list of DSST exams to determine which ones are most relevant to the degree you are seeking and to your base of knowledge. Schedule an appointment with your college adviser to determine which exams best fit your degree program and which college courses the DSST exams can replace. Advisers should also be able to tell you the minimum score required on the DSST exam to receive university credit.

DSST® TEST CENTERS

You can find DSST testing locations in community colleges and universities across the country. Check the DSST website (**www.getcollegecredit. com**) for a location near you or contact your local college or university to find out if the school administers DSST exams. Keep in mind that some universities and colleges administer DSST exams only to enrolled students. DSST testing is available to men and women in the armed services at more than 500 military installations around the world.

HOW TO REGISTER FOR A DSST® EXAM

Once you have located a nearby DSST testing facility, you need to contact the testing center to find out the exam administration schedule. Many centers are set up to administer tests via the internet, while others use printed materials. Almost all DSST exams are available as online tests, but the method used depends on the testing center. The cost for each DSST exam starts at $100, and many testing locations charge a fee to cover their costs for administering the tests. Credit cards are the only accepted payment method for taking online DSST exams. Credit card, certified check, and money order are acceptable payment methods for paper-and-pencil tests.

Test takers are allotted two score reports—one mailed to them and another mailed to a designated college or university, if requested. Online tests generate unofficial scores at the end of the test session, while individuals taking paper tests must wait four to six weeks for score reports.

PREPARING FOR A DSST® EXAM

Even though you are knowledgeable in a certain subject matter, you should still prepare for the test to ensure you achieve the highest score possible. The first step in studying for a DSST exam is to find out what will be on the specific test you have chosen. Information regarding test content is located on the DSST fact sheets, which can be downloaded at no cost from **www.getcollegecredit.com**. Each fact sheet outlines the topics covered on a subject-matter test, as well as the approximate percentage assigned to each topic. For example, questions on the Introduction to Business exam are distributed in the following way: Foundations of Business—20%, Functions of Business—60%, Contemporary Issues—20%.

In addition to the breakdown of topics on a DSST exam, the fact sheet also lists recommended reference materials. If you do not own the recommended books, then check college bookstores. Avoid paying high prices for new textbooks by looking online for used textbooks. Don't panic if you are unable to locate a specific textbook listed on the fact sheet; the textbooks are merely recommendations. Instead, search for comparable books used in university courses on the specific subject. Current editions are ideal, and it is a good idea to use at least two references when studying for a DSST exam. Of course, the subject matter provided in this book will be a sufficient review for most test takers. However, if you need additional information, then it is a good idea to have some of the reference materials at your disposal when preparing for a DSST exam.

Fact sheets include other useful information in addition to a list of reference materials and topics. Each fact sheet includes subject-specific sample questions like those you will encounter on the DSST exam. The sample questions provide an idea of the types of questions you can expect on the exam. Test questions are multiple-choice with one correct answer and three incorrect choices.

The fact sheet also includes information about the number of credit hours that ACE has recommended be awarded by colleges for a passing DSST exam score. However, you should keep in mind that not all universities and colleges adhere to the ACE recommendation for DSST credit hours. Some institutions require DSST exam scores higher than the minimum score recommended by ACE. Once you have acquired appropriate reference materials and you have the outline provided on the fact sheet, you are ready to start studying, which is where this book can help.

TEST DAY

After reviewing the material and taking practice tests, you are finally ready to take your DSST exam. Follow these tips for a successful test day experience.

1. **Arrive on time.** Not only is it courteous to arrive on time to the DSST testing facility, but it also allows plenty of time for you to take care of check-in procedures and settle into your surroundings.
2. **Bring identification.** DSST test facilities require that candidates bring a valid government-issued identification card with a current photo and signature. Acceptable forms of identification include a current driver's license, passport, military identification card, or state-issued identification card. Individuals who fail to bring proper identification to the DSST testing facility will not be allowed to take an exam.
3. **Bring the right supplies.** If your exam requires the use of a calculator, you may bring a calculator that meets the specifications. For paper-based exams, you may also bring No. 2 pencils with an eraser and black ballpoint pens. Regardless of the exam methodology, you are NOT allowed to bring reference or study materials, scratch paper, or electronics such as cell phones, personal handheld devices, cameras, alarm wrist watches, or tape recorders to the testing center.
4. **Take the test.** During the exam, take the time to read each question-and-answer option carefully. Eliminate the choices you know are incorrect to narrow the number of potential answers. If a question completely stumps you, take an educated guess and move on—remember that DSSTs are timed; you will have 2 hours to take the exam.

With the proper preparation, DSST exams will save you both time and money. So join the thousands of people who have already reaped the benefits of DSST exams and move closer than ever to your college degree.

INTRODUCTION TO BUSINESS EXAM FACTS

The DSST® Introduction to Business exam consists of 100 multiple-choice questions that cover the foundations and functions of business. The exam focuses upon the following topics: economic issues, international business, government and business, business ownership, entrepreneurship and franchise, management process, human resource management, production and operations, marketing management, financial management, risk management and insurance, and management and information systems. Careful reading, critical thinking, and logical analysis will be as important as your knowledge of business practices.

Area or Course Equivalent: Introduction to Business
Level: Lower-level baccalaureate
Amount of Credit: 3 Semester Hours
Minimum Score: 400
Source: https://getcollegecredit.com/wp-content/assets/factsheets/IntroductionToBusiness.pdf

I. Foundations of Business – 20%

  a. Forms of Business Ownership

  b. Government and Business

  c. Economics of Business

II. Functions of Business – 60%

  a. Management

  b. Marketing

  c. Finance

  d. Accounting

  e. Production and Operations

  f. Management Information Systems

  g. Human Resources

  h. Entrepreneurship

III. Contemporary Issues – 20%

  a. Internet and Social Media

  b. Business Ethics and Social Responsibility

  c. Global Business Environment

Chapter 2

Introduction to Business Diagnostic Test

DIAGNOSTIC TEST ANSWER SHEET

1. Ⓐ Ⓑ Ⓒ Ⓓ
2. Ⓐ Ⓑ Ⓒ Ⓓ
3. Ⓐ Ⓑ Ⓒ Ⓓ
4. Ⓐ Ⓑ Ⓒ Ⓓ
5. Ⓐ Ⓑ Ⓒ Ⓓ
6. Ⓐ Ⓑ Ⓒ Ⓓ
7. Ⓐ Ⓑ Ⓒ Ⓓ

8. Ⓐ Ⓑ Ⓒ Ⓓ
9. Ⓐ Ⓑ Ⓒ Ⓓ
10. Ⓐ Ⓑ Ⓒ Ⓓ
11. Ⓐ Ⓑ Ⓒ Ⓓ
12. Ⓐ Ⓑ Ⓒ Ⓓ
13. Ⓐ Ⓑ Ⓒ Ⓓ
14. Ⓐ Ⓑ Ⓒ Ⓓ

15. Ⓐ Ⓑ Ⓒ Ⓓ
16. Ⓐ Ⓑ Ⓒ Ⓓ
17. Ⓐ Ⓑ Ⓒ Ⓓ
18. Ⓐ Ⓑ Ⓒ Ⓓ
19. Ⓐ Ⓑ Ⓒ Ⓓ
20. Ⓐ Ⓑ Ⓒ Ⓓ

INTRODUCTION TO BUSINESS DIAGNOSTIC TEST
24 minutes—20 questions

Directions: Carefully read each of the following 20 questions. Choose the best answer to each question and fill in the corresponding circle on the answer sheet. The Answer Key and Explanations can be found following this Diagnostic Test.

1. A cafeteria benefits plan provides employees with

   A. an incentive to work harder.
   B. an opportunity to receive certain benefits on a pretax basis.
   C. reduced price lunches.
   D. the option of either selecting a profit-sharing plan or a merit salary plan.

2. What is the targeted market segment for the magazine *Popular Science*?

   A. Geographic
   B. Age
   C. Interest
   D. Income level

3. Which of the following describes a drop shipper?

   A. It inventories goods, sets up displays in stores, and bills for goods that are sold.
   B. It passes orders on to a manufacturer or another wholesaler and receives a commission.
   C. It inventories goods and sells directly to retailers.
   D. It inventories, sells, and delivers goods.

4. Which of the following is an example of public relations?

   A. Thirty-second ad on a TV show
   B. Personal appearance by an actor to promote a movie
   C. Press release about a new product
   D. Fan website for a TV show

5. What does SWOT stand for?

    A. Sweat equity, weaknesses, opportunities, threats
    B. Strengths, weaknesses, opportunities, threats
    C. Standards, wariness, optimism, threats
    D. Software, web, opportunities, technology

6. Which of the following describes the time value of money concept?

    A. The time value of money is a reason to invest in certificates of deposit.
    B. The value of money increases or decreases depending on inflation.
    C. Through investing, money will grow over time by earning interest.
    D. It is better to pay off debts with future money than with current money because inflation cheapens the value of money over time.

7. Which of the following is the most common form of business ownership in the United States?

    A. Sole proprietorship
    B. Partnership
    C. Limited liability partnership
    D. Corporation

8. Which of the following systems adds value to all businesses involved in producing goods from raw materials to finished product?

    A. Distribution channel
    B. Quality improvement team
    C. Supply chain management
    D. Organizational analysis

9. The second step in effective decision-making is to

    A. evaluate alternative solutions.
    B. choose one solution and execute it.
    C. generate alternative solutions.
    D. evaluate how well the solution is working.

10. Insider trading directly violates ethical conduct toward

A. other employees of the company.
B. investors in the company.
C. the company's customers.
D. the company's creditors.

11. Which of the following measures the market value of goods and services produced within a country during a year?

A. GDP
B. GNP
C. CPI
D. PPI

12. A US tech company hires a company in Ireland to handle its help line. The US company is

A. not focused on customer care as a goal.
B. entering into a partnership with the Irish company.
C. outsourcing work.
D. offshoring a part of its business.

13. Which of the following affect the demand for a product?

I. Changes in consumer preferences
II. The price of substitute goods
III. Decrease in the number of suppliers for the raw materials in the product

A. I only
B. I and II only
C. II and III only
D. I, II, and III

14. A major risk to companies that shift manufacturing to other countries is

A. the shuttering of their factories domestically.
B. home country import quotas.
C. the risk of political instability in host countries.
D. the high price of foreign labor.

15. Buying the latest smartphone because everyone in your group has one illustrates what type of influence on consumer behavior?

A. Personal
B. Sociocultural
C. Psychological
D. Demographic

16. A company's extranet is available to

A. anyone using the internet.
B. employees, customers, and vendors.
C. employees and customers.
D. employees only.

17. Among other traits, an affiliative leadership style

A. uses top-down management.
B. inspires employees.
C. is collaborative.
D. encourages goodwill and harmony among employees.

18. An example of direct marketing is a(n)

A. department store.
B. electronic storefront.
C. Tupperware® party.
D. manufacturer's representative calling on a chain store buyer.

19. Unemployment that is caused by a lack of demand for workers because of conditions in the economy is

A. seasonal unemployment.
B. cyclical unemployment.
C. structural unemployment.
D. frictional unemployment.

20. eBay® is an example of what type of e-commerce?

A. Business to business
B. Consumer to business
C. Business to consumer
D. Consumer to consumer

ANSWER KEY AND EXPLANATIONS

1. B	**5.** B	**9.** C	**13.** B	**17.** D
2. C	**6.** C	**10.** B	**14.** C	**18.** B
3. B	**7.** A	**11.** A	**15.** B	**19.** B
4. A	**8.** C	**12.** C	**16.** B	**20.** D

1. **The correct answer is B.** Cafeteria benefits plans are designed to reduce the costs of employee benefits. Employers can offer a variety of benefits, and employees can pick and choose as needed. Employees who participate contribute a portion of their gross income on a pretax basis. Choice A is incorrect because benefits don't depend on performance. Reduced priced lunches (choice C) are known as subsidized lunches. Choice D is incorrect because neither a profit-sharing plan nor a merit salary plan are matters of employee choice; both are determined by company policy.

2. **The correct answer is C.** The market segment for *Popular Science* is probably based on an interest in things scientific. Geographic region (choice A), age (choice B), and income level (choice D) are not likely to be influences on a purchase that doesn't depend on living in a certain region, being in a certain age range, or having a certain income level.

3. **The correct answer is B.** A drop shipper doesn't inventory the goods that it sells; it passes the orders that it takes on to the manufacturer or another wholesaler and receives a commission. Choice A describes a rack jobber. Choice C describes a cash-and-carry wholesaler. Choice D describes a truck wholesaler.

4. **The correct answer is A.** Only a prepared ad is an example of public relations. Choices B, C, and D are examples of publicity, where the company has no control over what is said or shown. Even the press release may not be used in the manner in which the company wants.

5. **The correct answer is B.** SWOT stands for strengths, weaknesses, opportunities, threats.

6. **The correct answer is C.** In addition to earning interest, money may yield other returns, such as dividends and stock splits. While it is true that the time value of money is a reason to invest in CDs, choice A is incorrect because this does not define the concept, which is what the question is asking. Choices B and D are true of inflation.

7. **The correct answer is A.** Sole proprietorship is the most common form of business ownership in the United States, making up about three quarters of US businesses, but only about 5 percent of business revenue. Corporations (choice D) make up about 20 percent of US businesses.

8. **The correct answer is C.** The key word here is *value*. Supply chain management adds value. A distribution channel (choice A) moves a product from raw materials to finished good. It does not provide value. A quality improvement team (choice B) operates within a single company to improve the quality of its processes and products. Organizational analysis (choice D) is a review of strengths and weaknesses conducted within a single company.

9. **The correct answer is C.** Step 1 is to identify the problem and step 2 is to generate alternatives. This has to be done before evaluating alternative solutions (choice A). Step 4 is to choose one of those alternatives and implement it (choice B). Step 5 is to evaluate how well the solution is working (choice D).

10. **The correct answer is B.** Insider trading is buying or selling stock based on confidential information about a company and can directly harm investors, either by driving down the price of the stock through selling or driving up the price of the stock through buying, putting it out of the range of an average investor. The key word here is *directly*. Insider trading may indirectly harm other employees (choice A), customers (choice C), and creditors (choice D) if the stock price dives and investors and lenders lose confidence in the business. However, this represents indirect, not direct, damage.

11. **The correct answer is A.** GDP stands for gross domestic product and is defined as the market value of all goods and services produced within a country during a year. GNP (choice B) stands

for gross national product and includes the value of all goods and services produced by facilities owned by domestic companies but located anywhere in the world. CPI (choice C) stands for consumer price index and refers to a market basket of goods and services that is monitored monthly for changes in its prices. PPI (choice D) is the producer price index and is the industrial equivalent of the CPI.

12. **The correct answer is C.** Outsourcing means giving work that was handled internally to an outside company, typically a company based in another country, whereas offshoring (choice D) is sending part of a company to another country. Choice A is incorrect because hiring a company in another country to provide customer service is not an indication that the company is not interested in offering good follow-up services to its customers post-purchase. Choice B is incorrect because the question states that the US company is hiring another company; there is no mention of any kind of partnership arrangement.

13. **The correct answer is B.** Items I and II are both factors that affect demand, whereas item III is a factor that affects supply.

14. **The correct answer is C.** Outsourcing work to other countries or building plants in other countries is risky if the country has a history of political unrest or repressive government. Choice A is not a risk to a company moving production offshore, though it may be a possibility or even a certainty. Choice B is incorrect because products made by or for a home country company on foreign soil don't come under import regulations when the goods are being shipped to the company's home country; import quotas govern goods made by foreign companies with no affiliation to a home country company. Choice D is incorrect because a major reason that companies shift manufacturing offshore is the low cost of labor in other countries.

15. **The correct answer is B.** Buying something because one's peers are buying it illustrates sociocultural influences on consumer behavior. A personal influence (choice A) would be buying a cheap phone because the buyer is always losing phones.

A psychological influence (choice C) includes perception, motivation, learning, and experience. Demographic (choice D) is a way to segment the market, not an influence on a consumer purchase.

16. **The correct answer is B.** A company's extranet is available to employees and to customers and vendors who are authorized to gain access. Choice A describes public sites on the internet. Choice C is too narrow of an answer because it omits vendors. Choice D describes a company's intranet.

17. **The correct answer is D.** An affiliative leadership style encourages goodwill and harmony among employees. Choice A describes an authoritarian leadership style. Choice B describes a visionary style of leadership, where leaders inspire employees. Choice C describes a democratic style.

18. **The correct answer is B.** Direct marketing, or direct response marketing, is direct contact between the seller and the buyer. A department store (choice A) is not an example of direct marketing. Choices C and D are examples of direct selling, not direct marketing.

19. **The correct answer is B.** The high unemployment rate during and after the recession of 2007 to 2010 was a result of cyclical unemployment; the unemployed were willing and able to work, but businesses were not hiring because of economic conditions. Seasonal unemployment (choice A) is unemployment tied to changes in season. Structural unemployment (choice C) is unemployment due to changes in an industry that may result from technological changes or changes in market demand. Frictional unemployment (choice D) is temporary unemployment that results when people change jobs or relocate.

20. **The correct answer is D.** eBay® enables consumers to sell to one another.

DIAGNOSTIC TEST ASSESSMENT GRID

Now that you've completed the diagnostic test and read through the answer explanations, you can use your results to target your studying. Find the question numbers from the diagnostic test that you answered incorrectly and highlight or circle them below. Then focus extra attention on the sections dealing with those topics.

Introduction to Business		
Content Area	Topic	Question #
Foundations of Business	• Forms of business ownership • Government and business • Economics of business	7, 11, 13, 19
Functions of Business	• Management • Marketing • Finance • Accounting • Production and operations • Management information systems • Human resources • Entrepreneurship	1, 2, 3, 4, 5, 6, 8, 9, 15, 16, 17, 18
Contemporary Issues	• Internet and social media • Business ethics and social responsibility • Global business environment	10, 12, 14, 20

Chapter 3

Introduction to Business Subject Review

FOUNDATIONS OF BUSINESS

Every business produces a good or a service or both. How it produces its product is determined by a number of factors. Before even those decisions are made, however, a businessperson will need to decide what type of business they want to establish. Depending on the answer, the new business owner(s) will need to fill out government forms, pay taxes in a certain way, and follow certain rules and regulations pertinent to the business. Underpinning all this is the economics of conducting business.

Forms of Business Ownership

There are five basic forms of business ownership:

1. Sole proprietorship
2. Partnership
3. Co-operative
4. Corporation
5. Nonprofit corporation types

Partnerships and corporations have several different formats.

Sole Proprietorship

The sole proprietorship is the most common form of business ownership in the United States, accounting for almost three quarters of the business organizations in the country. Anyone who runs a business alone is a sole proprietor unless that person has incorporated the business. No paperwork or special reporting to the IRS is required of sole proprietorships. Sole proprietorships are run by one person, but that person may hire employees.

There are a number of advantages to the sole proprietorship form of business ownership: lack of legal requirements for establishing and operating the business, low start-up costs, no separate tax filings so the owner gets all the benefit of any tax loss, no need to divide any profits, and no shared decision making. However, some of these benefits may also be a disadvantage. For example, without a partner, there is no one with whom to share losses. Other disadvantages include unlimited liability, difficulty in borrowing money, responsibility for all losses, no one to share in making decisions, and the end of the business when the owner retires or dies.

The major disadvantage is **unlimited liability**, that is, the sole proprietor is held responsible for all debts that the business incurs, as well as all liabilities. For example, if a plumber doesn't turn off the water before installing a new toilet and water floods the bathroom and leaks to the first floor, the homeowner could sue the plumber for damages. If the plumber is a sole proprietor and the homeowner wins, the homeowner could go after the plumber's savings and home to satisfy the judgment. A sole proprietor who employs others is responsible for them as well when it comes to liability. It is also difficult to borrow money to set up or expand a sole proprietorship because a bank will only lend based on the owner's assets.

Partnership

In forty-eight of the fifty states, a partnership must file information about the business under the federal **Revised Uniform Limited Partnership Act**. However, partnerships are similar to sole proprietorships in that no separate business tax filings are required. An important advantage of a partnership over a sole proprietorship is that the former will find it easier to borrow money for the business from banks. In a partnership, the business doesn't rest on the ability of just one person to make it grow. Other advantages include all partners share in contributing to the start-up costs, in any profits, and in decision making.

The most important disadvantage to partnerships is unlimited liability. In a partnership, each partner is responsible not only for their own debts and actions in the course of conducting the business but also for whatever the other partners incur in the course of doing business.

There are two types of partnerships: general and limited. The description so far of a partnership describes the **general partnership** arrangement. In a **limited partnership**, some partners are investors only and have no decision-making authority over the operations of the business. The liability of limited partners is equal only to the percentage of the business they own. A partnership that has limited partners must have at least one general, or active, partner. This person manages the business on a day-to-day basis and has unlimited liability.

TIP: All partnership agreements should establish at the beginning the responsibilities of all partners and the guidelines for the addition and departure of partners over time.

Co-operative

Another form of business ownership is the **co-operative**, which is a group of partnerships and/or sole proprietorships that join together to benefit their individual businesses. As a group, they have more financial power than as individual businesses and, therefore, have greater bargaining power for things such as reduced rail rates for shipping goods. Co-operatives are more common in agriculture than in other industries.

Corporation

A **corporation** is formed according to state laws. It is an entity that is separate from its owners, the stockholders, and thus has liability separate from its owners. It must file corporate tax returns annually and has certain legal rights, such as the ability to sue, and certain legal obligations, such as obedience to the law. Unlike the other forms of business ownership, a corporation raises capital by selling shares in its business. The liability of investors, or stockholders, in a corporation is limited; their liability extends only to the amount of their investment in the corporation.

In addition to limited liability for investors, the advantages of a corporate form of business ownership are ease of obtaining capital and continuity of management. The future growth and management of a corporation doesn't depend on one person—unless the corporation is really a one-person operation formed for liability purposes. A major disadvantage of corporations is double taxation. The profits of a corporation are taxed as business income, and when they are paid out as dividends, stockholders must pay tax on them as personal income.

Corporations are owned by their investors. Overall governance falls to a board of directors, but day-to-day operations are overseen by the officers of the corporation, typically a chief executive officer (CEO) and a chief financial officer (CFO). Sometimes, the CEO is a chief operation officer (COO) instead.

There are six types of corporations:

1. *Privately or Closely Held:* The founding family, a group of investors, or the employees of the company may hold the shares. Outsiders cannot buy stock. Profits are taxed as corporate income and shareholders have limited liability.
2. *Public or Publicly Held (also known as a C Corp):* Any member of the public and employees can buy stock. Profits are taxed as corporate earnings, and shareholders have limited liability.
3. *Subchapter S (commonly called an S Corp):* Shareholders pay personal income tax on their share of any profits that the business earns. S corps don't pay corporate taxes, but they must file tax returns annually. Shareholders have limited liability.
4. *Limited Liability (LLC):* Profits are taxed as personal income and shareholders enjoy limited liability.
5. *Professional:* These are formed by professionals such as lawyers and doctors and enjoy limited liability.
6. *Multinational or Transnational:* These corporations have operations in multiple countries and their stock is sold on multiple stock exchanges. Regulations, including taxes, vary from country to country.

Nonprofit Corporation

A **nonprofit**, or **not-for-profit**, is typically set up to support a social or educational mission. A not-for-profit, as the name implies, doesn't make a profit. Any revenue that it generates that isn't required for operations is used to further its mission. Nonprofits are tax-exempt if they qualify under federal regulations, but they must file a tax return and fulfill other reporting requirements for the federal government and for the states under which they operate.

Government and Business

Government influences the business climate in two ways: through regulatory policy and through economic policy. Governments—federal, state, and municipal—regulate what businesses can and cannot do. Through their tax policies, all three levels of government affect how much money businesses have to spend and can borrow. The federal government also affects businesses through monetary policy.

Regulatory Policies

State and local governments have a variety of rules and regulations that affect businesses, from requiring licenses for companies to do business to collecting city wage taxes on suburban commuters. These are statutory laws, which are made by state legislatures and, therefore, vary from state to state. For example, some states require that companies of a certain size carry disability insurance on their employees, but other states do not. Some have **right-to-work laws** forbidding closed shops, and other states don't. However, when many think of "government," they think of the federal government and its regulatory reach. Every aspect of business is covered under some department or agency of the federal government. For example:

- **Department of Labor:** The Bureau of Labor Statistics compiles a number of economic indices to aid businesses and workers, such as the Occupational Safety and Health Administration (OSHA).
- **Department of Agriculture (USDA):** In addition to overseeing farm subsidy programs, the USDA supports the Women, Infant, and Children (WIC) food assistance program, as well as other child nutrition programs.
- **Department of Health and Human Services:** The Food and Drug Administration (FDA) oversees food safety programs and approves new drugs before they can be sold in the United States.
- **Department of Commerce:** According to its website, the US Department of Commerce has "a wide range of responsibilities in the areas of trade, economic development, technology, entrepreneurship and business development, environmental stewardship, and statistical research and analysis." Commerce oversees patents and trademarks, imports and exports, and manufacturing standards.
- **Federal Trade Commission (FTC):** The FTC is a separate agency of the federal government, not affiliated with an executive branch-level department. The agency's mission includes consumer protection as well as the advancement of competition. Deceptive advertising practices come under its jurisdiction, as do the Telemarketing Sales Rule, the Pay-Per-Call Rule, and the Equal Credit Opportunity Act.

TIP: Other independent agencies related to business are the Consumer Product Safety Commission (CPSC), the Environmental Protection Agency (EPA), and the National Transportation Safety Board (NTSB).

Businesses, regardless of their size, are subject to a variety of laws, including the following:

- **Contract:** To be valid, a contract must include a stated offer and acceptance, have mutual consent, include a consideration (exchange of item of value, such as a dollar), be legal, and be in the proper form depending on the amount and term of the contract.
- **Tort:** A wrongful act or an infringement of a right; includes intentional infliction of distress, negligence, financial loss, injury, and invasion of privacy
- **Property:** Includes intellectual, tangible real, tangible personal, or intangible personal property
- **Agency:** Governs those who act for another party
- **Commercial:** Also known as mercantile law or trade law; Governs business, commerce, and consumer transactions; includes the Uniform Commercial Code, contracts, and warranties
- **Bankruptcy:** Federal laws, including Chapter 7, (liquidation) and Chapter 11 (reorganization)

Fiscal and Monetary Policies

One aspect of federal economic policy is the maintenance of a stable economic environment in which businesses can operate. As you will read below, economies go through fluctuations known as **business cycles**. The federal government, through fiscal and monetary policies, seeks to smooth out these ups and downs in output, unemployment, and inflation.

Fiscal policy refers to taxes and government spending. With the exception of some fees, the federal government—like state and local governments— raises revenue through levying taxes on businesses and individuals. When inflation is rising, raising taxes can cool down the economy. The higher the taxes, the less money there is for consumers to buy goods and services and the slower the economy. When the economy is in a downturn, cutting taxes doesn't have the opposite effect. Some people will use the additional money for new spending as the government intends, but some will pay off old debts, and others will save the additional money. Another way to stimulate the economy in a downturn is to increase government spending. Rather than increase taxes, the government borrows money by selling Treasury bonds, notes, and bills for varying periods of time and at competitive market rates.

Monetary policy is the tool of the **Federal Reserve System**, commonly referred to as the Fed, which is an independent agency. The Fed is the nation's central bank, or banker's bank, and as such, operates the twelve district banks of the Federal Reserve System, oversees member banks in those districts, and sets the nation's general money and credit policies. It has three tools that it can use:

1. *Discount Rate:* The rate charged to member banks to borrow money. Used as a tool to keep inflation in check. A higher discount rate translates to less money the banks will borrow, which results in less money being lended, thus slowing the economy. The lower the discount rate is, the more money banks will borrow, the more they will lend, and the more the economy will grow.
2. *Reserve Requirement:* The amount of funds that a bank must hold in reserve to ensure that it is able to meet its liabilities in the case of sudden withdrawals. This requirement acts similarly to the increases and decreases in the discount rate.
3. *Open-Market Operations:* A mechanism to buy or sell bonds and securities on the open market. Buying puts money into the economy to stimulate it and selling takes money out of the economy to contract it.

Economics of Business

Economics, as defined by Merriam-Webster's dictionary, is "the science that deals with the production, distribution, and consumption of wealth and with the various related problems of labor, finance, taxation, etc." It almost sounds like a definition of business. Businesses try to accurately discern the needs, wants, and desires of the marketplace in order to produce and distribute the right mix of goods, or products, while dealing with labor, financial issues, competition, and the like.

A company may operate in any one of four types of economic systems:

1. *Traditional:* Rural, agrarian economy of which few still exist
2. *Planned:* Control by the government over what is produced, how, and for whom and at what price; complete control under a communist system and a lesser degree of control in a socialist system; in the latter, typically government-run social services and utilities
3. *Market:* Decisions about what to produce, how, for whom, and at what price made by businesses and individuals; free market, free enterprise, capitalist systems
4. *Mixed:* Combination of planned and market systems; economic decisions made by businesses and individuals with some government control and oversight; examples include the United States, Great Britain, and Germany

Regardless of the type of economic system, there are five factors of production in play: labor, natural resources, capital, entrepreneurs, and technology. Capital is divided into real capital, meaning the equipment and facilities used to produce goods and services, and financial capital, the money needed to start up and operate a business.

Economics of Supply and Demand

In a **market economy** or **mixed economy**, such as the United States, market forces set prices through the laws of supply and demand. Demand is the willingness and ability of consumers to buy a good or service, and supply is the willingness and ability of producers to produce a good or service. The law of supply states that producers will offer more of a product/service as the price increases and less of a product/service as the price decreases. The law of demand works in reverse. Consumers will buy more of a product/service as the price decreases and less of a product/service as the price increases.

The point at which a balance between supply and demand is reached is called the **equilibrium point** or, in business terms, the **market price**. Supply and demand are shown on supply curves and demand curves. A **supply curve** indicates the amount of goods or services offered at different price points, and a **demand curve** shows how many products or services will be bought at different price points. When there is more demand than supply, a shortage occurs. When there is more supply than demand, a surplus occurs.

A variety of factors can affect both supply and demand and thus the availability and price of goods and services. Factors affecting supply, positively or negatively, may be changes in the price of raw materials, forecasts of future prices—either up or down, acceleration of technological change, increase or decrease in the number of competitors, and increase or decrease in the price of substitute goods. Demand may be changed positively or negatively by such factors as increase or decrease in income distribution, changes in consumer preferences, changes in population age and distribution, and increase or decrease in demand for substitute goods.

Competition

Competition is one characteristic of market and mixed economies. The other three are the right to own property, freedom of choice in buying and selling goods and services and one's labor, and profits. There are various degrees of competition from none to complete, or perfect, competition:

- **Monopoly:** Lack of competition; single supplier of a good or service, or one dominant supplier in an industry; controls pricing
- **Monopolistic:** Several producers making similar products that are perceived as slightly differentiated; no perfect substitute goods; each producer can set own price within certain limits of the marketplace; mix of large and small businesses competing for market share
- **Oligopoly:** Few producers, little differentiation of product, little difference in pricing; occurs in industries with high barriers to entrance, such as large initial investment costs, well-established firms, fierce competition
- **Perfect:** Many producers—large and small; no perceived differences by consumers among products; pricing set by the marketplace

Economic Indicators

To be successful, those who run businesses must be aware of the economic environment in which they operate. **Aggregate output** is the total amount of goods and services produced by an economy in a given period. There are a number of indicators that show how well or how poorly the economy is doing. The federal government regularly compiles and publishes many of these reports. Among the indicators are the following:

- **Gross Domestic Product (GDP):** Total value of all goods and services produced domestically in a given period; no goods and services produced outside the country are included
- **Gross National Product (GNP):** Total value of all goods and services produced by a nation's companies regardless of where the facilities are located in a given period of time; considered a less accurate indicator of an economy's health than GDP
- **Consumer Price Index (CPI):** Based on a market basket of goods and services that doesn't vary from month to month in order to show a pattern of monthly expenses for the typical urban household; the eight categories are food, housing, clothing, transportation, medical care, recreation, education, and miscellaneous items, such as haircuts and cigarettes
- **Producer Price Index (PPI):** Measurement of selling prices received by domestic producers of goods and services for their products, includes prices for raw materials, component goods, and finished goods
- **Unemployment Rate:** Low rate can translate into difficulty finding qualified workers; high rate can indicate low consumer demand
- **Productivity:** Rate at which goods and services are produced in a given period; output per capita; the higher the productivity, the healthier the economy

Two other important numbers that affect a nation's economy are the national debt and the balance of trade. To raise money to pay its bills, the federal government sells bonds in addition to levying and collecting taxes. The more bonds the government sells, the more money it takes out of the general pool of investor dollars, which makes it more difficult for businesses—large and small—and individuals to borrow. The balance of trade may affect the economy positively or negatively. If a country sells more goods abroad than it imports, the balance of trade is positive. If the opposite is true, the balance of trade runs a trade deficit. The country owes more to other countries than it takes in from exports.

Over time, the economy goes through peaks and valleys—expansions and contractions—that are known as **business cycles**. Expansions are known as booms; severe contractions are called depressions and less severe contractions are called recessions. In addition, the economy can be affected by inflation, when price levels across the economy rise, and deflation, when price levels across the economy decline. The federal government, through its fiscal and monetary tools, attempts to even out these ups and down with stabilization policies. The aim of the polices is (1) to keep prices in check in order to slow inflation and (2) to expand demand in order to lower unemployment.

Unemployment rate can be affected by several factors and categorized into four types:

1. *Cyclical unemployment*, in which the unemployed are willing and able to work, but businesses are not hiring because of economic conditions. The high unemployment rate during and after the recession of 2007 to 2010 was an example of cyclical unemployment.
2. *Seasonal unemployment*, which is unemployment tied to changes in season, such as construction workers who have no work in the winter and ski instructors who are unemployed in the summer.
3. *Structural unemployment*, which is unemployment due to changes in an industry that may result from technological changes or changes in market demand; for example, the loss of jobs by typewriter repairers when computers replaced typewriters.
4. *Frictional unemployment*, which is temporary unemployment resulting from people changing jobs or careers or relocating.

FUNCTIONS OF BUSINESS

What types of organization are used currently in companies? What makes a good manager? How are prices set? What financial controls should a company have? How do information systems make companies more efficient? This section answers these questions and more as it describes the varied functions of business.

Management

As Ebert and Griffin's *Business Essentials* defines management, it "is the process of planning, organizing, leading, and controlling an organization's financial, physical, human, and information resources to achieve its goals." Planning is an essential element of the role of management and includes setting the goals, strategies, and tactics for the business. The function of control includes monitoring the business' performance and making adjustments as needed if goals are not being met.

Management is divided into three levels:

1. *Top managers* run the overall organization.
2. *Middle managers* see that the company's strategies are implemented and goals are being met.
3. *First-line managers* directly oversee employees.

Organizations have a number of functional areas in common: financial, human resources, information, marketing, and operations. Depending on the industry, an organization may have additional functional areas, such as research and development (R&D) or strategic alliances.

Managers need certain skills, including the following:

- **Technical:** The specialized skills required for a particular industry and series of jobs within that industry
- **Interpersonal:** The ability to interact with and motivate employees. It's more than the ability to get along with people and includes the ability to communicate effectively and inspire confidence, loyalty, and good work
- **Decision Making:** The ability to identify problems, gather and evaluate information, develop alternative solutions, evaluate alternatives, and select the best one for the problem; the plan is then subjected to further evaluation to determine if it met its goals

- **Conceptual:** The ability to think in the abstract, to see the big picture; extremely useful in SWOT analysis (strengths, weaknesses, opportunities, threats), where the first two concepts are internal factors and the last two are external to the organization
- **Time Management:** Using time for one's self and one's subordinates most efficiently and effectively, includes prioritizing paperwork, establishing agendas for meetings, setting aside a time for phone calls, and organizing and prioritizing emails for response

In addition to these skills, many managers today will need to be able to manage in a global environment, which requires understanding of the global business environment and understanding of cultural differences with foreign nationals within their own companies and with strategic partners and competitors. The ability to conceptualize the use of technology for efficient operations and communication is also important.

Planning

Organizations develop five types of plans: strategic, tactical, operational, contingency, and crisis.

1. *Strategic plans* set the future of the organization. An extremely important function of managers, especially top management, this type of planning encompasses developing a vision statement and a mission statement, conducting a SWOT analysis, establishing goals, developing objectives, and determining tactics to achieve the objectives and goals, ultimately creating the vision. The primary focus is on long-range goals.
2. *Tactical plans* are carried out by middle managers with the oversight of top managers. These plans involve intermediate goals—from one to five years.
3. *Operational plans* are typically developed by middle managers and first-line managers based on short-range goals that can range from daily to quarterly.
4. *Contingency plans* help a company deal with unexpected changes that significantly impact operations. For example, a significant jump in gasoline prices that causes consumers to buy smaller, more fuel-efficient cars, forcing car makers to change their car designs and produce smaller, more fuel-efficient cars.
5. *Crisis management plans* detail how an organization will continue to operate during an emergency, such as 9/11.

Organizing

Organizing a company is determining how the company will be structured. **Structure** is determined by specialization of tasks, departmentalization of those specialties/tasks, and distribution of decision making. Typically, the three levels of management in large businesses are organized in a structure resembling a pyramid, with top-level management at the top, and first line managers at the bottom.

Within this structure, there are three types of organizational frameworks possible, based on the distribution of authority: horizontal, vertical, and network. The horizontal structure flattens out the pyramid. This type of structure decentralizes authority among various levels of management within the organization, including line departments, staff, and committees and teams. The vertical structure centralizes authority in top-line management. A network structure combines one or more organizations to produce a good or provide a service. This often involves either forming a partnership for a specific venture, or outsourcing such items as marketing, production, and/or sales.

Leading

Part of a manager's job is to motivate, encourage, and influence others. There are a variety of approaches to leadership as identified by researchers: trait, behavioral, situational, transformational, and charismatic. Motivation may be extrinsic or intrinsic. There are three main theories about motivation:

1. *Maslow's Hierarchy of Needs:* From lowest to highest: physiological, safety, belonging, esteem, self-actualization
2. *Herzberg's Motivator-Hygiene Theory or Two Factor Theory:* Hygiene translates into basic features such as pay and benefits, company policy and administration, relationships with coworkers, supervision, status, job security, working conditions, and personal life. Motivators include achievement, recognition, the work, responsibility, promotion, and growth.
3. *McClelland's Three Needs Theory:* Needs for achievement, affiliation, power

Controlling

Management establishes and oversees the controls necessary to ensure that the business is working toward and achieving its goals. The basic categories of controls are bureaucratic, market, and clan—that is, the mutual sense of benefit that employees gain from working together.

Marketing

The concept of marketing has evolved through four stages since the earliest product marketing in the Industrial Revolution. These stages are production, sales, marketing, and relationship.

Marketing strategies have two components: **target market** and **marketing mix**. The product, price, promotion, and place—known as the Four P's of marketing—comprise the marketing mix, where place refers to distribution. An integrated marketing strategy merges the elements of the marketing mix so that the Four P's are presented as a coherent whole to the marketplace.

Marketing Process

The first step in the marketing process may begin before there is even a product to sell: identifying a market need. Market research helps identify the need and how to fulfill it and also identifies the target market. The next step is to develop a marketing plan that includes a SWOT analysis, the target market, the product, and how it will be produced, priced, promoted, and distributed. Once the groundwork has been laid, the team can begin to implement the plan and then assess the effectiveness.

Market segmentation is an important part of identifying a target market. Market segments may be geographic, demographic, psychographic (lifestyles, personality traits, motives, and values), and behavioral (benefits sought, volume use, brand loyalty, price sensitivity, and product end use).

Consumer and B2B Marketing

A variety of influences affect consumer behavior: psychological, personal, social, cultural, situational, and marketing mix. The process that consumers undertake in making buying decisions includes need/problem recognition, information search, evaluation of alternatives, purchase decision, and post-purchase evaluation.

Business-to-business (B2B) marketing is different from marketing to consumers because business buyers are trained professionals who specialize in purchasing. They are not consumers in a nonbusiness marketplace who know little about the industry. Buyers and sellers in the B2B market develop close relationships over time that facilitate purchasing.

Consumer goods and services are classified as convenience, shopping, specialty, and unsought. B2B goods and services are categorized as equipment; maintenance, repair, and operating (MRO); raw and processed materials; components; and professional services.

Product

Without products—goods or services or both—a company will have nothing to sell, and unless a company is a start-up or sells to a niche, a company will sell a group of products known as its product mix. A **product mix** is made up of a number of product lines, all the products, including peripherals, which serve a similar need for customers.

Consumer goods and services can be classified as convenience (e.g., milk and bread), shopping (e.g., subject of some comparison shopping because of price), and specialty (e.g., a prom dress). Goods for the B2B market can be classified as expense or component and capital.

Products go through a life cycle: introduction, growth, maturity, and decline. During the growth phase of a product, competitors begin to introduce their own products to compete. During the maturity stage, the company may look upon the product as a cash cow, putting little money into new developments for the product in return for a higher profit. In doing this, a company is attempting to maximize profits and defend market share at the same time.

Branding and packaging are two important aspects of marketing a product. **Branding** is the use of a name, slogan, symbol, social media strategy, or design to differentiate a company and its products from its competitors. The intent of a company's branding activities is to generate brand recognition, brand preference, and, ultimately, brand insistence. There are several types of brands: generic, manufacturer's or national, private, family, individual, licensed, and co-branding. **Licensing** takes place when a company or person sells the right to use its name or logo to another company for use on its products, such as the Italian designer Valentino's selling the right to use his name to a French fashion house. **Co-branding** occurs when two companies put both their names on the same product, such as the Intel logo on Lenovo computers.

Packaging is important because it safeguards the product, is meant to discourage stealing, promotes the product/brand, lists features and benefits, and may add utility. Considering the emphasis on being "green" today, it should also be environmentally friendly to appeal to certain customers.

Price

Product pricing depends on the goal of the company, which may be to maximize profits, build market share, build traffic, maximize sales, and/or foster an image, for example, low prices for value or high prices to denote quality. The major strategies for pricing are:

- **Cost-Based**, or **Cost-Plus:** Based on the cost of manufacturing/offering the product
- **Demand-Based**, or **Value-Based:** Based on the demand for or perceived value of the product in the marketplace
- **Competition-Based:** Pricing influenced by what the competition is charging
- **Price Skimming:** For new products; an initial high price to recoup costs associated with development and introduction of the product; high-profit margin
- **Penetration Pricing:** For new products; an initial low price to introduce a product to the market and begin to generate market share

Pricing is also affected by price adjustments like discounts; rebates; product bundling (so that the combined price is lower than the single price of each item); psychological, or fractional pricing, which prices items at less than a whole dollar ($1.99); and loss leaders, which lower the price on one or more sale items to bring customers into the store.

Promotion

Promotion is all the techniques that companies use to get the message to the marketplace about their products. The promotional mix includes advertising; personal selling; sales promotions like cents-off discount coupons, bounce-back coupons, and point-of-sale (POS) displays; and publicity and public relations. To ensure a clear, coherent, and unified message for all contacts with customers, companies use an integrated marketing communication strategy.

Once a target market has been identified and objectives determined, a marketing manager or product manager develops the product's "message," determines the appropriate media mix (including social media networks) to get the message out, develops the budget, launches the campaign, and assesses the effectiveness of the campaign, revising as needed.

Place

Place is actually places; it's the distribution aspect of marketing. **Distribution** is made up of distribution channels that take products from raw materials to buyer. Distribution may involve intermediaries between the producer and end user: wholesalers who buy from producers and resell to other intermediaries or to end users, retailers who sell directly to end users, and agents and brokers.

Unlike wholesalers and retailers, agents and brokers do not purchase the products they sell; they act on behalf of the buyer or seller, depending on the type of agent or broker. Agents and brokers are paid a commission, rather than making a profit on their deals, and may be manufacturer's agents, selling agents, or purchasing agents.

There are four distribution channels:

> *Channel 1—Direct:* producer to consumer or business

> *Channel 2—Retail:* producer to retailer to consumer or business

> *Channel 3—Wholesale:* producer to wholesaler to retailer to consumer or business

> *Channel 4—Broker or Agent:* producer to broker or agent to consumer or business

There are a variety of retailers, with both physical and virtual presences:

- **Brick-and-Mortar Retailers:** department stores, supermarkets, specialty stores, convenience stores, discount/bargain stores, wholesale/warehouse clubs, factory outlets, catalog showrooms
- **Direct Response Retailers:** catalog mail order, telemarketing
- **E-tailers:** e-catalogs, virtual storefronts

TIP: Assets are defined as everything a company owns, including any cash on hand, investments, equipment, and real estate.

Finance

A company's financial management is responsible for the planning and budgeting of funding for both its short-term and long-term operations, including research and development and capital investments. Monitoring cash flow is an important part of the job of financial management. Having adequate cash flow ensures that creditors can be paid, but it also means that the company's invoices are being paid in a timely manner. Oversight of receivables and payables falls under the umbrella of financial management.

To ensure that short-term needs are met, financial managers in collaboration with department heads prepare an operating budget for the organization. Long-term needs, including capital projects, for example, the purchase of new technologies or large-scale equipment, are provided for in a capital budget. Whereas operating expenses should be paid for out of revenue, capital expenditures may be financed by borrowing money, selling a new block of stock, or issuing corporate bonds.

Using the proceeds from the sale of stock is called **equity financing**. Issuing bonds to raise capital is called **debt financing**. There are two types of **bonds: unsecured** and **secured**, also known as **debenture bonds**. An unsecured bond is backed only by the promise to repay the full value of the bond with interest at a stated time in the future.

Even short-term financial needs may require borrowing to balance cash out with cash in. Small businesses may be able to satisfy their needs with a bank line of credit or with a commercial loan; corporations more typically sell unsecured commercial paper. A commercial loan may or may not be secured by a company's assets, which include any cash on hand, investments, equipment, and real estate. The creditworthiness of the business typically determines whether the borrower qualifies for an unsecured loan.

The **gross profit margin** determines the overall profitability of a company's production. It indicates the overall efficiency of the organization in using its resources—both human and material. Gross profit margin equals total revenue minus cost of goods sold divided by total revenue.

Accounting

Accounting is the recording, analysis, and reporting of the financial transactions of a business, which includes all its income (accounts receivable) and expense (accounts payable) activities. The following are different types of accounting:

- In **managerial accounting**, staff track the costs of doing business and the resulting income, monitor the profitability of various business activities, and develop budgets. The audience is typically comprised of internal managers.
- In **financial accounting**, the focus is on preparing documents that show the financial performance of a company. The audience is those outside the company, such as stockholders.

- In **audit accounting**, the focus is on reviewing a company's financial documents to ensure their accuracy and reliability. Reviews may be completed by internal accountants and/or by outside auditors.
- In **tax accounting**, staff advise on tax strategies and help to prepare tax returns.

The financial reports that accountants prepare for businesses typically consist of balance sheets, income statements, and cash flow. Each contains different kinds of information about a company's financial health or lack thereof:

- **Balance Sheet:** Shows current assets, fixed assets, short-term liabilities, long-term liabilities, and owner's equity. Assets may also be intangible, like trademarks, patents, and goodwill.
- **Income Statement:** Shows revenues, cost of goods sold, gross profit, operating expenses, operating income, and net income.
- **Cash Flow Statement:** Shows cash from operations, investments, and financing.

Financing cash flow statements includes both inflows of cash from debt and equity financing, as well as outflows in the form of interest and dividend payments and repayment of principle borrowed.

Accountants must follow **GAAP standards** (generally acceptable accounting principles) in preparing and reviewing financial reports. All financial reporting starts with bookkeeping and is based on the accounting equation:

$$\text{Assets} = \text{Liabilities} + \text{Owner's Equity}$$

Owner's equity is what the business is worth if the owner chose to sell it. The owner would get whatever was left after the liabilities were deducted from the assets. Assets minus liabilities is the net worth of a business.

Production and Operations

Operations include all the activities that go into producing products; operations management is the control of those activities. **Products** may be tangible goods or intangible services. **Services** are also "unstorable"; you can't store the cheerful, helpful attention of a waiter in a restaurant. Production results in three types of utility, or value, for customers: form (what customers need), time (when customers need it), and place (where customers need it).

There are a variety of processes that companies use to make goods and services and a variety of ways of classifying them. Three typical processes are (1) mass, (2) flexible, also known as custom, and (3) customer-driven. The first is the traditional assembly-line process instituted by Henry Ford at the beginning of the twentieth century. In a flexible system, a central computer operates a network of machines and can adjust product specifications and output as needed. The first two are typical make-to-stock operations and the last is a make-to-order operation. Service operations are classified as low-contact or high-contact, depending on the amount of involvement of the customer in the process.

Ford's assembly line was among the first uses of technology to speed and improve manufacturing. The most noticeable technology on the manufacturing floor today is the presence of robots. However, while they do many of the manufacturing processes that humans once did, humans still control the type and flow of work. Other processes that employ technology are computer-aided design (CAD), computer-aided manufacturing (CAM), and computer-integrated manufacturing (CIM).

A number of factors need to be managed in order to establish smooth-running operations. These include determining optimum number, size, and location of facilities; optimum number of employees; proximity of facilities to transportation networks, utility grids, and suppliers; and design of the facility.

Once facilities are up and running, operations managers are responsible for the timely flow of materials through production to final goods and into the distribution channel, so part of the planning for smooth-running operations is scheduling and controls. Controls on the operations side include inventory control and quality control. **Inventory control** consists of all the activities involved in receiving, storing, and tracking whatever the business uses to produce its goods—for example, raw materials—as well as the finished goods. Two popular methods of materials management among large corporations are **materials requirement planning (MRP)** and **enterprise resource planning (ERP)**. Both use technology for planning/scheduling and inventory control, but ERP integrates them into the overall business. Two methods for tracking production processes are PERT (Program Evaluation and Review Technique) charts and Gantt charts (named after chart designer Henry Gantt).

A business's quality control methods and activities include establishing what "quality" means in its environment and monitoring goods and services to ensure that they provide that quality. It is not simply a matter of maintaining the same level of quality, but of improving that quality over time. With a process known as **total quality management (TQM)**, companies attempt to infuse quality into the entire production process from the first design of a product to follow-up service after the product has been delivered to the customer. With TQM, ensuring quality becomes the mission of every employee in a company.

The **International Organization for Standardization (ISO)** establishes global standards for what constitutes quality. It has two programs worldwide: ISO 9000 certification and ISO 14000 certification. The latter certification attests to the company's development of an environmental management system.

Management Information Systems

Management information systems (MIS) is one part of the technology side of a business. **Information technology (IT)** is the overall umbrella label for a company's technology systems, and it is overseen by the chief information officer (CIO) in large corporations. The IT department designs and implements all computer-based information systems in a company, whereas MIS uses technology to collect and analyze data, and use the resulting information to inform decisions and solve problems.

The shift from data to information occurs when the surveys, statistics, facts—whatever has been collected—are analyzed, arranged, and interpreted. The data that the business collects are stored in what is called a **data warehouse**. Analyzing the data to find trends and patterns is called **data mining**.

There are different kinds of information systems software: decision support systems, executive information systems, knowledge information systems, and business intelligence. Knowledge information systems software is used by knowledge workers to create new types of information based on manipulating data. The other three systems provide data and models to help various levels of management in different departments make informed decisions.

Companies face any number of threats to their information systems because of access to the internet. Businesses may find themselves and their customers the victims of hackers, intellectual property theft, identity theft, spyware, viruses, Trojan horses, worms, and spam. Firewalls, encryption software that encodes email, spam-filtering software, antivirus protection, and antispyware protection are ways to defend against hackers and malicious attacks on networks.

In addition to doing business over the internet, large companies have intranets that are closed to all but their own employees and extranets that are available to employees, customers, and vendors who are authorized to gain access. Companies use social media to connect with customers. Some companies are also creating work and process groups on their own social media sites to exchange information.

Human Resources

The human resources department is a vital part of an organization, responsible for recruiting and training employees, developing compensation and benefits packages, and developing a system for evaluating employees. Many companies consider HR a strategic partner in planning future goals and objectives for achieving those goals.

Recruiting and Hiring

HR is responsible for job analysis within an organization and then creating job descriptions and job specifications for open positions. Recruiting to fill those jobs may be external or internal. External sources of candidates are online job sites; networking, both online and offline; career fairs; hiring headhunters to recruit employees away from competitors; newspaper and trade journal ads; employment agencies; and referrals.

A number of federal laws regulate **hiring practices**. Title VII of Civil Rights Act of 1964 prohibits discrimination based on race, color, national origin, gender, religion, and retaliation ("for opposing unlawful employment practices, for filing a complaint, for testifying about violations or possible violations"). In addition, the Age Discrimination Act prohibits age discrimination against anyone over the age of 40 in companies with 20 or more employees. Discrimination against those with disabilities is prohibited by the Americans with Disabilities Act, and discrimination against those who take a leave to serve in one of the uniformed services is prohibited by the Uniformed Services Employment and Reemployment Rights Act. Claims of discrimination are handled by the Equal Employment Opportunity Commission (EEOC).

A variety of issues and events have transformed the workplace and workforce in the early twenty-first century. Companies are making more of an effort to diversify and be inclusive so that their workforce mirrors their markets. With each succeeding technological innovation, the importance of data has increased, resulting in an increased demand for "knowledge workers", such as software engineers and developers, computer programmers, accountants, and financial analysts. In an effort to keep costs down and employ talent on a project basis, employers are hiring contract workers, contingent workers, and gig workers, which include part-time, temporary, seasonal, and leased employees.

Training and Evaluation

The initial training that employees undergo is typically a half- or full-day orientation on a company's rules and regulations, history, and corporate culture. During the course of employment, workers also receive additional training—on the job, in an apprentice program, at off-site sessions, or through distance learning. Training programs deal with the here and now, whereas development programs take the long view and help employees learn skills that will help them grow in their jobs and the organization.

Performance appraisals assess how employees are doing their jobs. They include a self-assessment as well as an assessment of the employee by their manager or supervisor. The assessment is conducted against a set of standards that includes the goals set by the employee and manager in the previous performance appraisal. Employee assessments occur at regular intervals, usually once a year, but can occur prior to a promotion or on an ongoing basis.

Compensation and Benefits

Wages are paid for hourly work, and salaries are paid for a specific job. Some employees, specifically salespeople, may work on commission only or on a combination of salary and bonus. Workers may be exempt or nonexempt, depending on how jobs are classified under the Fair Labor Standards Act.

Employers of nonexempt workers must abide by the law. These workers must be paid at least the federal minimum wage and receive overtime pay for working more than a regular workweek, which is typically 40 hours.

There are exceptions to the minimum wage law, for example, tipped employees, full-time students, workers under 20 years of age, and workers with disabilities. An employer must follow the guidelines regarding limits on how far below the minimum wage they are legally allowed to pay workers, and wages may be subject to increase if the worker's circumstances change.

Many companies offer retirement plans to their employees. Types of retirement plans include defined contribution plans, 401(k) plans, profit sharing, and employee stock ownership plans (ESOP). The amount an employee is allowed to contribute is dependent upon the type of plan available and the length of time the employee has been with the company.

Companies must carry workers' compensation insurance by law. They must also offer adequate minimum health care coverage to qualifying employees. Other benefits offered may include paid time off, paid sick leave, tuition reimbursement, supplemental insurance, scholarships to children of employees, child care, and wellness programs.

Many companies offer a cafeteria benefits plan, where employees can choose from a variety of pretax benefits. These plans allow employers to offer a better selection of benefits to their employees, while helping to offset rising costs.

To provide more of a work-life balance, and to also cut facility costs, some companies have chosen to offer alternative work arrangements such as flex-time, telecommuting, permanent part-time work, job sharing, and/or compressed work weeks. Advancements in technology and the internet have created an opportunity for many jobs to be completed remotely, or on a hybrid work schedule. The benefits to these work arrangements include greater flexibility and productivity, lower absence rates, and higher job satisfaction.

Termination

Perhaps the hardest aspect of an HR professional's job is terminating employees. Sometimes terminations occur because of poor performance, but other times it may be the result of an economic downturn for the company or for the economy as a whole. Employees who lose their jobs through no fault of their own are laid off rather than fired and typically given severance packages that may be based on one or two weeks for each year of employment. They are also eligible for unemployment compensation.

Employees who are fired are not eligible for unemployment and do not receive severance. Terminating an employee for cause requires following a process: a verbal warning and the opportunity to remedy the problem, written warning and the opportunity for remediation, and then termination if performance has not improved. Even though most workers fall under the category of "employment at will," the process is still followed.

Labor Unions

Labor union contracts are built on the principle of collective bargaining. Management of a company sits down with representatives of the union to work through a set of compromises to come up with a contract. If agreement cannot be reached, there are several options: work slowdown, sickout, and strike. A strike is accompanied by a picket line and sometimes by a boycott of the company's product by a sympathetic portion of the public. A company may bring in strikebreakers to take over the strikers' work. To end the impasse, the union and the company may agree to the use of a mediator or to binding or nonbinding arbitration.

Entrepreneurship

Ford didn't start out as a multinational corporation, neither did Apple®. Both companies began with one or two individuals and an idea, and, from that idea, the founders went on to produce a product and launch a business. They were entrepreneurs, individuals willing to take risks. Various characteristics are ascribed to entrepreneurs, such as being innovative, resourceful, risk-takers, flexible, self-motivated, able to work well with others, good leaders, and able to see the "big picture." The desire to be one's own boss also plays a role in entrepreneurship. Some entrepreneurs start their own businesses because they want to make a comfortable living, want more control over their lives, or want the flexibility that comes with owning their own business, whereas others start their businesses with the intention of making it as large and profitable as possible. The former are the owners of small businesses, the majority of US companies, and the latter are the start-ups looking for sizable infusions of venture capital.

While many entrepreneurs start businesses based on their own idea, some choose instead to buy an existing business. The risks are more or less known, there is an existing base of customers and suppliers, and there is a financial history to use as the basis for projections of future financial performance. For the same reasons, other entrepreneurs choose to buy franchises. The franchiser also provides its expertise in helping the franchisee set up the business and training and marketing, including advertising materials. The downsides to a franchise are the cost of buying the franchise license, the associated start-up costs, the percentage that the franchisee pays the franchiser, the lack of creativity and control over the individual business, and the competition from similar national brands.

The first step for both types of entrepreneurs is creating a business plan that includes goals and objectives, a sales forecast, and a financial plan indicating income, the break-even point, and a budget. Securing funding is the next big hurdle. Typically, a small business is funded with the owner's savings and loans or investments from family and friends. Other forms of funding include venture capital companies, small business investment companies (SBIC), angel investors (individuals rather than companies), and various programs of the Small Business Administration (SBA), including 7(a) loans, special purpose loans, micro loans, and the Certified Development Company (504) loan program.

Four main reasons for small business success are (1) competent management, (2) commitment to doing whatever it takes to succeed, (3) accurate reading of demand in the marketplace for the product or service, and (4) being in the right place at the right time with the right product, or luck. Some of the reasons for small business failures include (1) lack of planning upfront before the business is set up, (2) inexperienced or incompetent management, (3) lack of commitment to the business, (4) weak financial and inventory controls, and (5) lack of enough capital to support the business until it becomes profitable.

CONTEMPORARY ISSUES

Companies—whether multinationals or sole proprietorships—face a number of issues in today's business environment. Among them are the internet and social media, business ethics and social responsibility, and the global business environment.

Internet and Social Media

Merriam-Webster defines the **internet** as "an electronic communications network that connects computer networks and organizational computer facilities around the world." The internet makes it possible to communicate and do business from anywhere in the world, at any time, without having a physical presence.

Social media is an internet-based form of communication. The following are the different forms of social media:
- Blogging and publishing networks
- Consumer review networks

- Content creation and bookmarking networks
- Discussion forums
- Media sharing networks
- Social networks

E-commerce is the business of buying and selling electronically. Transactions may be with another business, or may be in the form of direct sales to consumers. The latter, known as **e-tailing**, has several forms: online auctions, e-catalogs, electronic storefronts (websites), electronic or cyber malls (collection of sites), and interactive marketing on blogs and social media sites.

Using the internet and social media for business purposes can be very powerful. Advantages of the internet include potential access to global markets, reduced marketing costs and overhead, and automated systems and resource sharing. Social media can help a company engage with its audience, increase website traffic, generate leads, boost sales, and build relationships.

However, there are a number of risks associated with an increased online presence. Negative reviews can have a devastating effect on credibility and sales. No matter how secure a website may be, sites can be hacked, and customers' personal information stolen. The result is identity theft and millions of dollars lost through the use of stolen information. Companies may encounter issues related to fraud, trademark or copyright infringement, system reliability, search engine optimization (SEO), and customer disputes.

Business Ethics and Social Responsibility

Ethics is a set of moral beliefs, a code of conduct based on what is considered right and wrong. Living an ethical life does not stop at the workplace door. Part of an organization's culture is its ethical stance on issues, which can be found in a company's code of ethics, mission statement, and legal compliance. Ethical behavior within a company includes doing right by fellow employees, customers, suppliers, and the organization itself. The organization in turn has a responsibility to treat employees, customers, suppliers, and other business partners ethically.

Social responsibility is the belief that organizations as well as individuals are obligated to act in such a way as to benefit the larger society. Corporate social responsibility (CSR) institutionalizes this belief on a company-wide basis.

Areas of concentration for CSR activities include human rights; employees and other stakeholders, including customers, the larger community, and the environment; and ethical business practices related to sourcing, producing, and marketing. The last includes recognizing consumer rights, disavowing deceptive advertising practices, and using fair pricing practices.

The benefits of CSR include:

- **Less government intervention into business practices** because the organization is obeying all applicable legislation and regulations
- **Better financial performance** as a result of efficient use of resources, including people, and an enhanced perception in the marketplace
- **Fewer scandals** related to corruption and fewer accidents, thereby reducing the company's exposure to risk
- **Competitive edge with customers** by advertising CSR programs, including philanthropic endeavors
- **Easier recruitment of employees** because they embrace the company's CSR initiatives
- **Higher rate of employee retention** for the same reason

Some companies may adopt any one of four approaches to CSR, from embracing it wholeheartedly to doing as little as possible:

1. *Obstructionist Stance:* Do as little as possible to solve the problems that it creates; deny or hide any responsibility
2. *Defensive Stance:* Do what is legally required, admit mistakes, remedy the problem to the letter of the law only, defend the stance that the job of the company is to generate profits
3. *Accommodative Stance:* Meet ethical obligations and legal requirements; participate in social programs, but do not seek them out
4. *Proactive Stance:* Seek out opportunities to support social programs, perception as "citizens of society"

How well a company is living up to its CSR can be measured by taking a social audit in which the company's performance is measured against its goals. Some companies choose to make this information public. A **benefit corporation**, or **B corporation**, is a for-profit corporate entity authorized by 21 states and the District of Columbia that is required to consider the impact of its business decisions both on shareholders and the environment and society.

Some businesses go so far as to become certified for benefiting society. A for-profit company that obtains a **B Corp certification** has met certain standards of social and environmental performance, accountability, and transparency as outlined by B Lab, a global nonprofit organization.

Another public expression of CSR is **corporate philanthropy**. Some corporations set up charitable foundations to donate money to worthy causes, thereby living up to their goals to support the larger community. A number of outside groups such as Boston College's Center for Corporate Citizenship and *Fortune* magazine also rate and rank corporations on their CSR programs.

Global Business Environment

Business ethics and CSR extend across borders when doing business. The **globalization** of the world's economies affects workers, consumers, businesses, unions, the environment, and national governments—and even state governments. Some states send trade representatives to other countries in an effort to encourage foreign companies to establish facilities in their states. The increase in the rate of globalization in the last two decades is a result of changes in technology and the lowering of trade barriers.

Globalization impacts both markets and production. A market for a company's products could be consumers in China as well as Chicago. With outsourcing of production, factories producing the components for smartphones could be spread across Asia. **Cultural differences** come into play in conducting market research and developing, advertising, and selling products in multiple markets.

Cultural differences also affect the production process. A cultural difference that can lead to legal difficulties—and ethical ones—is the issue of bribery. Some nations consider it business as usual if a company wants to operate within their borders. However, the US Foreign Corrupt Practices Act of 1977, the Anti-Bribery Convention of the Organization for Economic Cooperation and Development, and the UN Convention Against Corruption all prohibit bribery of foreign officials. In addition to cultural differences, companies doing business across borders must deal with economic, legal, and political environments that vary not only from their home country but also from country to country worldwide.

Trade Policies

Countries seek to have a favorable balance of trade, that is, having the value of exports be greater than the value of imports. This situation results in a favorable balance of payments, which is when a country takes in more revenue than it pays out. When this occurs, the country has a **trade surplus**. The opposite is a **trade deficit**.

One issue that can constrain businesses is **protectionist trade policies**— their own country's and that of countries with which they wish to do business. A protectionist trade policy uses quotas and tariffs to protect domestic industries by making foreign goods more expensive to import. A home country may also use subsidies as a way to protect domestic producers. Instead of limiting imports as a quota does or raising prices as a tariff does, a subsidy is a payment to domestic producers to enable them to keep their prices lower than those charged by importers of the same or similar goods.

Those in favor of protectionist trade policies use the following arguments to support their position:

- **Infant Industry:** Newly emerging domestic industries need to be protected from foreign competition
- **National Security:** Industries vital to the nation's security need to be protected so that foreign competitors do not undercut them on price or the nation will find itself dependent on the foreign companies
- **Foreign Labor:** Companies in developing nations will undercut domestic companies by using cheap labor to produce their goods
- **Bargaining Chip:** A tough trade policy can be used to negotiate with trading partners to get them to relax their trade policies

Dumping is selling goods abroad for less than they cost to make or are sold for domestically. Charges of dumping can be brought to the World Trade Organization for resolution.

....

TIP: Some countries have local content laws that require a product be made at least in part in the country where it will be sold.

....

Regional and International Organizations

There are a variety of organizations that promote free trade. Among them are the World Trade Organization (WTO), General Agreement on Tariffs and Trade (GATT), European Union (EU), North American Free Trade

Agreement (NAFTA), MERCOSUR (Brazil, Argentina, Paraguay, Uruguay), and Association of Southeast Asian Nations (ASEAN).

Absolute and Comparative Advantage

A nation has an **absolute advantage** when it produces more of a product more cheaply than any other country. **Comparative advantage** occurs when a nation can produce a product more efficiently than any other country. Therefore, it should concentrate on producing that product and buying from other countries the products that they have comparative advantage in. Comparative advantage is competitive advantage.

Ways to Enter Foreign Markets

A company wishing to enter a foreign market has a variety of paths to choose from. It can simply hire an import agent who deals with customs, tariffs, and selling the company's goods. A company can enter into a deal with a domestic company by selling a franchise or license. It can enter into a joint venture or strategic alliance, or, depending on the type of company, it can set up a turnkey project for which it will be paid but will have no ownership stake in when finished. Another arrangement for a manufacturing company is contracting out its manufacturing to a company in the country it wishes to enter. Any type of company could set up a wholly owned subsidiary.

SUMMING IT UP

- The basic forms of business ownership are **sole proprietorship**, **partnership**, and **corporation**. There are also **co-operative and nonprofit** corporation forms of businesses.
  - The **sole proprietorship** is the most common form of business ownership in the United States. Advantages include lack of legal requirements for establishing and operating the business, low start-up costs, no separate tax filings, no need to divide any profits, and no shared decision making. The disadvantages are unlimited liability, difficulty in borrowing money, responsibility for all losses, no one to bounce ideas off of, and the end of the business when the owner retires or dies.
  - In a **partnership**, no separate business tax filings are required, it is easier to borrow money from banks, all partners contribute to start-up costs, and all partners participate in decision making. A disadvantage is that any profits are divided as well, but the most important disadvantage is unlimited liability. Partnerships may be general or limited.

- ⊚ A **corporation** is formed according to state laws; is an entity that is separate from its owners, the stockholders; has liability separate from its owners; must file corporate tax returns annually; and has certain legal rights.
- ⊚ In a **co-operative**, a group of partnerships and/or sole proprietorships join together to benefit their individual businesses.
- ⊚ A **nonprofit**, or **not-for-profit**, is set up to support some social or educational mission.
- Government influences the business climate in two ways: through **regulatory policy** and through **economic policy.**
- Businesses are subject to **contract, tort, property, agency, commercial**, and **bankruptcy laws.**
- One aspect of federal economic policy is the **maintenance of a stable economic environment in which businesses can operate.** This is the **goal of the Federal Reserve System's monetary policy.**
- **Entrepreneurs** may start a business based on their own idea, buy an existing business, or buy a franchise.
- A **franchiser** provides expertise, training, and marketing. The disadvantages of buying a franchise are the cost of buying the franchise license, start-up costs, the percentage the franchisee pays the franchiser, lack of creativity and control over the business, and competition from similar national brands.
- There are **five factors of production:**
  1. labor
  2. natural resources
  3. capital (real and financial)
  4. entrepreneurs
  5. technology
- In a **market economy**, or **mixed economy**, market forces set prices through the laws of supply and demand.
  - ⊚ The **law of supply** states that producers will offer more of a product/service as the price increases and less of a product/service as the price decreases. The **law of demand** states that consumers will buy more of a product/service as the price decreases and less of a product/service as the price increases.
  - ⊚ The characteristics of market and mixed economies are competition, private property rights, freedom of choice in buying and selling goods and services, and profits.
- Economic indicators are **gross domestic product (GDP), gross national product (GNP), consumer price index (CPI), producer price index (PPI), unemployment rate,** and **productivity**.
- **Management** plans, organizes, leads, and controls the financial, physical, human, and information resources of an organization.

- **Planning** is an essential element of management and includes setting the goals, strategies, and tactics for the business.
  - The **function of control** includes monitoring the business's performance and making adjustments as needed if goals are not being met.
  - There are a variety of **approaches to leadership** as identified by researchers: **trait, behavioral, situational, transformational,** and **charismatic. Motivation** may be extrinsic or intrinsic.
- Marketing strategies have two components: **target market** and **marketing mix.**
  - **Product, price, promotion,** and **place**—the **Four P's of marketing**—comprise the marketing mix. The Four P's are presented as a coherent whole to the marketplace.
  - The promotional mix includes advertising; personal selling; sales promotions; publicity, including social media campaigns; and public relations.
- A company's **financial management** is responsible for the planning and budgeting of funding for both its short-term and long-term operations.
- **Accounting is the recording, analysis,** and **reporting of a business's financial transactions,** which includes all its income and expense activities—accounts receivable and accounts payable.
- **Operations include all the activities that go into producing products;** operations management is the control of those activities. **Products** may be tangible goods or intangible services.
- **Management information systems (MIS)** use technology to collect and analyze data and use the resulting information to inform decisions and solve problems.
- The **human resources department** is responsible for recruiting and training employees, developing compensation and benefits packages, and developing a system for evaluating employees.
- **E-commerce** is the business of buying and selling electronically where the transaction may be between business and business or business and consumer.
- **Ethics** is a set of moral beliefs, a code of conduct based on what is considered right and wrong. Part of an organization's culture is its ethical stance on issues.
- **Social responsibility** is the belief that organizations as well as individuals are obligated to act in such a way as to benefit the larger society. **Corporate social responsibility (CSR)** institutionalizes this belief on a company-wide basis.
- **Globalization** impacts both markets and production.
- Some countries take a **protectionist approach** to their trade policies with the intent of protecting domestic industries from foreign competitors.

Chapter 4

Introduction to Business Post-Test

POST-TEST ANSWER SHEET

1. Ⓐ Ⓑ Ⓒ Ⓓ
2. Ⓐ Ⓑ Ⓒ Ⓓ
3. Ⓐ Ⓑ Ⓒ Ⓓ
4. Ⓐ Ⓑ Ⓒ Ⓓ
5. Ⓐ Ⓑ Ⓒ Ⓓ
6. Ⓐ Ⓑ Ⓒ Ⓓ
7. Ⓐ Ⓑ Ⓒ Ⓓ
8. Ⓐ Ⓑ Ⓒ Ⓓ
9. Ⓐ Ⓑ Ⓒ Ⓓ
10. Ⓐ Ⓑ Ⓒ Ⓓ
11. Ⓐ Ⓑ Ⓒ Ⓓ
12. Ⓐ Ⓑ Ⓒ Ⓓ
13. Ⓐ Ⓑ Ⓒ Ⓓ
14. Ⓐ Ⓑ Ⓒ Ⓓ
15. Ⓐ Ⓑ Ⓒ Ⓓ

16. Ⓐ Ⓑ Ⓒ Ⓓ
17. Ⓐ Ⓑ Ⓒ Ⓓ
18. Ⓐ Ⓑ Ⓒ Ⓓ
19. Ⓐ Ⓑ Ⓒ Ⓓ
20. Ⓐ Ⓑ Ⓒ Ⓓ
21. Ⓐ Ⓑ Ⓒ Ⓓ
22. Ⓐ Ⓑ Ⓒ Ⓓ
23. Ⓐ Ⓑ Ⓒ Ⓓ
24. Ⓐ Ⓑ Ⓒ Ⓓ
25. Ⓐ Ⓑ Ⓒ Ⓓ
26. Ⓐ Ⓑ Ⓒ Ⓓ
27. Ⓐ Ⓑ Ⓒ Ⓓ
28. Ⓐ Ⓑ Ⓒ Ⓓ
29. Ⓐ Ⓑ Ⓒ Ⓓ
30. Ⓐ Ⓑ Ⓒ Ⓓ

31. Ⓐ Ⓑ Ⓒ Ⓓ
32. Ⓐ Ⓑ Ⓒ Ⓓ
33. Ⓐ Ⓑ Ⓒ Ⓓ
34. Ⓐ Ⓑ Ⓒ Ⓓ
35. Ⓐ Ⓑ Ⓒ Ⓓ
36. Ⓐ Ⓑ Ⓒ Ⓓ
37. Ⓐ Ⓑ Ⓒ Ⓓ
38. Ⓐ Ⓑ Ⓒ Ⓓ
39. Ⓐ Ⓑ Ⓒ Ⓓ
40. Ⓐ Ⓑ Ⓒ Ⓓ
41. Ⓐ Ⓑ Ⓒ Ⓓ
42. Ⓐ Ⓑ Ⓒ Ⓓ
43. Ⓐ Ⓑ Ⓒ Ⓓ
44. Ⓐ Ⓑ Ⓒ Ⓓ
45. Ⓐ Ⓑ Ⓒ Ⓓ

46. Ⓐ Ⓑ Ⓒ Ⓓ   51. Ⓐ Ⓑ Ⓒ Ⓓ   56. Ⓐ Ⓑ Ⓒ Ⓓ

47. Ⓐ Ⓑ Ⓒ Ⓓ   52. Ⓐ Ⓑ Ⓒ Ⓓ   57. Ⓐ Ⓑ Ⓒ Ⓓ

48. Ⓐ Ⓑ Ⓒ Ⓓ   53. Ⓐ Ⓑ Ⓒ Ⓓ   58. Ⓐ Ⓑ Ⓒ Ⓓ

49. Ⓐ Ⓑ Ⓒ Ⓓ   54. Ⓐ Ⓑ Ⓒ Ⓓ   59. Ⓐ Ⓑ Ⓒ Ⓓ

50. Ⓐ Ⓑ Ⓒ Ⓓ   55. Ⓐ Ⓑ Ⓒ Ⓓ   60. Ⓐ Ⓑ Ⓒ Ⓓ

INTRODUCTION TO BUSINESS POST-TEST
72 minutes—60 questions

Directions: Carefully read each of the following 60 questions. Choose the best answer to each question and fill in the corresponding circle on the answer sheet. The Answer Key and Explanations can be found following this post-test.

1. What is the most common form of business ownership in the United States?

   A. Corporation
   B. Sole proprietorship
   C. Partnership
   D. Co-operative

2. Price skimming is used in which stage of the product life cycle?

   A. Introduction
   B. Growth
   C. Maturity
   D. Decline

3. Which of the following poses a question of social responsibility for a company?

   A. Price fixing
   B. Outsourcing
   C. Harassing a whistleblower
   D. Reporting inflated profits

4. Which of the following illustrates the concept of direct foreign investment?

   A. Opening a sales office in a foreign city
   B. Building a factory in a foreign country
   C. Licensing the use of technology to a foreign company
   D. Selling a business unit to a foreign company

5. The benefits that buyers receive from a product are categorized as what type(s) of utility?

   A. Time, form, and place
   B. Price, promotion, and place
   C. Form, time, place, and ownership
   D. Value

6. Which of the following information systems software allows users to create new types of information?

   A. Decision support
   B. Knowledge information
   C. Business intelligence
   D. Executive information

7. Which of the following is an example of corporate philanthropy?

   A. Sponsoring the Great American Cleanup
   B. Refusing to do business with a company that uses sweatshops
   C. Shifting to recycled packaging for a company's products
   D. A network's refusing to allow the product placement of cigarettes in a TV program

8. What is a major disadvantage of buying an existing business?

   A. Buying an existing business takes more time than setting up a new company.
   B. It can be easier to obtain financing for a start-up than to buy an existing business.
   C. There is little opportunity for creating a new look for the business or introducing new products.
   D. An existing business may have a poor reputation for customer service or product quality.

9. In which stage of a product's life cycle do competitors introduce rival products?

   A. Introduction
   B. Growth
   C. Maturity
   D. Decline

10. Which of the following is an accounting function in a company?

    A. Preparing income statements

    B. Investing a company's surplus funds

    C. Providing input for budgeting

    D. Determining whether to borrow money or issue stock to fund capital needs

11. Encryption software protects a company's email by

    A. filtering out spam.

    B. identifying and removing spyware.

    C. encoding messages so they can't be read without a passphrase to unscramble them.

    D. erecting a barrier to block messages unless told to recognize the sender.

12. Which of the following is an example of dumping?

    A. Manufacturers sell goods in a foreign country for less than what it cost to manufacture them.

    B. Clothing manufacturers cut up out-of-season clothes and trash them to clear inventory.

    C. Stores sell goods for less than what they paid in order to clear inventory.

    D. A foreign government offers a subsidy to domestic manufacturers that make and sell goods abroad to offset import duties.

13. Enterprise resource planning program (ERPP) software does which of the following?

    A. Helps entrepreneurs predict the potential for success

    B. Is an online performance appraisal system

    C. Connects all functions of a business operation such as inventory control, scheduling, finance, marketing, and human resources

    D. Is a tool for franchises

14. The Smith Company wants to enter the German market with its product and decides to establish the business with a German company. They are setting up what kind of business?

   A. Licensing
   B. Joint venture
   C. Strategic alliance
   D. Contract manufacturing

15. The airline industry, with its few competitors, could be characterized as

   A. an oligopoly.
   B. an industry with perfect competition.
   C. having monopolistic competition.
   D. a monopoly.

16. Which of the following is an example of a company exercising its corporate social responsibility?

   A. Returning an overpayment to a customer
   B. Conducting an audit of working conditions in a foreign factory producing components for its smartphones
   C. Turning over emails requested by a federal investigation into fraudulent dealings by a CFO
   D. Labeling food packaging with nutrition information

17. According to the principles of financial management, which of the following should be paid for through the issuance of corporate bonds?

   A. Research and development
   B. Operating expenses
   C. Interest payments on loans
   D. Construction of new facilities

18. Which of the following is a conceptual skill that managers need to be effective?

   A. Empathy
   B. Ability to use situation analysis
   C. Ability to implement plans
   D. Ability to fact find

19. Entrepreneurship and technology are increasingly important

    A. capital requirements.
    B. elements in the product mix.
    C. operations units.
    D. factors of production.

20. A flat organizational structure is most often found in a(n)

    A. decentralized organization.
    B. tall organization.
    C. centralized organization.
    D. autocratic organization.

21. Which of the following is an example of a shopping good?

    A. Computer tablet
    B. Wedding gown
    C. Doughnut and coffee
    D. Engagement ring

22. Which of the following is an internal environment that affects how companies do business?

    A. Cross-cultural environment
    B. Economic environment
    C. Corporate culture
    D. Political-legal environment

23. Net income is

    A. gross profit minus operating expenses and income taxes.
    B. gross profit minus operating expenses.
    C. assets minus liabilities.
    D. costs of materials used to produce goods during a given year.

24. An organization would typically write an intermediate goal for something it wished to accomplish

    A. in less than one year.
    B. in one year.
    C. within one to three years.
    D. within one to five years.

25. Currency depreciation causes

    A. imports to rise in price.
    B. imports to become cheaper.
    C. exports to rise in price.
    D. no effect on imports and exports.

26. A Gantt chart shows the

    A. structure of an organization.
    B. sequence of tasks that must be performed in order and the tasks that can be performed simultaneously with those tasks.
    C. steps in a project and time required to perform each step.
    D. products to be produced, their deadlines, and those who will be working on the projects.

27. Which of the following is a characteristic of business-to-business markets?

    A. Purchasing decisions are made by individual agents
    B. Lack of personal relationships between sellers and buyers
    C. Small number of customers
    D. Informal nature of the seller-buyer process

28. Businesses fail for which of the following reasons?

    I. Ineffective financial controls
    II. Lack of adequate capitalization
    III. Inexperienced management

    A. I only
    B. I and II only
    C. II and III only
    D. I, II, and III

29. The ISO 9000 label indicates that a company's products

    A. adhere to the highest quality.
    B. are environmentally safe.
    C. are manufactured in a socially responsible way.
    D. are organic.

30. In determining where to locate a manufacturing facility, a company needs to consider

A. inventory management.
B. the size of the market.
C. the availability of workers with appropriate skills.
D. creating an efficient layout for the facility.

31. A nation has a comparative advantage in a certain good when that country

A. can produce the good at a lower cost than other countries.
B. was the earliest producer of the product.
C. can produce the good more efficiently than other nations.
D. can produce a higher quality of the good.

32. Which of the following can be binding on both sides in a labor dispute?

A. Mediation
B. Arbitration
C. Collective bargaining
D. Boycott

33. A small business selling craft materials and needing money to balance out cash flow would most likely

A. sell a debenture.
B. sell unsecured commercial paper.
C. issue stock.
D. apply for a bank line of credit.

34. How is B2B e-commerce similar to traditional B2B selling?

A. The orders are small.
B. The customer base for a product is small.
C. There is decentralized purchasing.
D. Little or no comparison shopping is done among competitors.

35. The goal of US monetary policy is to

A. issue government debt at a favorable market rate.
B. collect revenue for the purpose of operating the government.
C. stabilize the economy.
D. safeguard money kept in depository institutions.

36. A balance sheet details a company's

    A. profit and loss.
    B. financial status.
    C. receipts and payments.
    D. assets, liabilities, and owner's equity.

37. Which of the following is an intrinsic motivator for employees?

    A. Profit-sharing plan
    B. Employee-of-the-month program
    C. Sense of achievement
    D. Promotion

38. Taking out a bank loan has an advantage over having an angel investor because

    A. a bank will make a loan to a partnership, but angel investors typically prefer to invest in sole proprietorships.
    B. a bank loan is paid off over time, whereas an angel investor is paid a share of the profits for as long as the business exists.
    C. a bank will act in an advisory capacity to the entrepreneur, whereas an angel investor takes a hands-off role.
    D. it means that the entrepreneur will still be eligible for an SBA loan.

39. Using an internet job site is what type of recruiting for a new hire?

    A. External
    B. Prospecting
    C. Internal
    D. Headhunting

40. Which of the following is a contingent worker?

    A. Call center employee
    B. Lawyer on lease
    C. Truck driver who owns and drives his own truck
    D. Daughter employed as a sales agent for the family construction company

41. An organization that changes and adapts to its environment is referred to as a

A. continuous improvement organization.
B. TQM organization.
C. learning organization.
D. flexible organization.

42. Statutory law is law

A. established by administrative agencies.
B. passed by state legislatures.
C. developed from court decisions.
D. based on court precedents.

43. The amount of goods and services that will be bought at all price levels at a given point in time is

A. the equilibrium point.
B. aggregate output.
C. aggregate demand.
D. real growth rate.

44. Which of the following are reasons that motivate people to become entrepreneurs?

I. Desire to control what they work at and how they do their work
II. Desire for flexibility in their lives
III. Desire to make more money

A. I and II
B. II only
C. I and III
D. I, II, and III

45. Employees who feel connected to the company and to their fellow employees most likely fall into which category in Maslow's hierarchy of needs?

A. Safety
B. Belonging
C. Esteem
D. Self-actualization

46. Software that is designed to disrupt a computer's operation is

    A. spyware.
    B. malware.
    C. spam.
    D. cookies.

47. Total revenue minus cost of goods sold divided by revenue equals

    A. operating expenses.
    B. operating profit margin.
    C. gross profit margin.
    D. earnings per share.

48. Jack's department is charged with analyzing data to find trends and patterns, which is known as

    A. data mining.
    B. data interpretation.
    C. data collection.
    D. data drilling.

49. Competition from goods manufactured in developing countries is used to support which of the following arguments for a protectionist trade policy?

    A. Bargaining chip
    B. Infant industry
    C. Cheap foreign labor
    D. National security

50. Which of the following is characteristic of a market economy?

    A. Government control of some industries and competition in others
    B. Central planning
    C. Low barriers to entry into industries
    D. The right to own property

51. To help new junior employees learn their jobs and adjust to the company culture, some companies

    A. make them part of a work team.
    B. enroll them in apprenticeships.
    C. assign them a mentor.
    D. give them an orientation program.

52. In backward scheduling, the operations department has to schedule

   A. according to supplier availability.
   B. based on input from the just-in-time inventory control system.
   C. based on when raw materials are due to arrive.
   D. based on when a product needs to be shipped.

53. In terms of assets, brand recognition and a company's reputation are classified as

   A. intellectual property.
   B. liquid assets.
   C. goodwill.
   D. tangible property.

54. Advertising, public relations, sales promotions, and personal selling are the components of which of the following?

   A. Four P's
   B. Promotional mix
   C. Media mix
   D. Product differentiation

55. To calculate net income, an accountant would need what information?

   I. Total revenue
   II. Total assets
   III. Total expenses

   A. I only
   B. I and II only
   C. I and III only
   D. I, II, and III

56. The role of the World Bank in global development is to

   A. rescue failing banks that are too big for their own governments to help.
   B. fund programs to improve conditions and increase productivity in developing nations.
   C. provide advice and technical expertise to nations to avert financial crises.
   D. develop monetary policy to stabilize the economy.

57. Which of the following is a true statement about the minimum wage?

  A. All hourly jobs are covered by the minimum wage.
  B. The Federal Fair Labor Standards Act mandates those jobs that must be paid the minimum wage.
  C. Violations of the minimum wage are investigated by the Employment Opportunity Commission.
  D. Any job that is negotiated by collective bargaining is not covered by the minimum wage.

58. Which of the following is an advantage to a business partnership over a sole proprietorship?

  A. Limited liability
  B. Greater ability than a sole proprietorship to borrow money to expand the business
  C. Less paperwork than a sole proprietorship to start the business
  D. Greater tax advantages to the owners than a sole proprietorship

59. What is a disadvantage to e-tailing for consumers?

  A. Comparison shopping is difficult.
  B. The product array is limited.
  C. The consumer cannot see and touch the product.
  D. Prices are higher than in brick-and-mortar stores.

60. Point-of-sale displays are an example of

  A. sales promotion.
  B. advertising.
  C. a distribution channel.
  D. an impulse buy.

ANSWER KEY AND EXPLANATIONS

1. B	13. C	25. A	37. C	49. C
2. A	14. B	26. C	38. B	50. D
3. B	15. A	27. C	39. A	51. A
4. B	16. B	28. D	40. B	52. D
5. C	17. D	29. A	41. C	53. C
6. B	18. B	30. C	42. B	54. B
7. A	19. D	31. C	43. C	55. C
8. D	20. A	32. B	44. D	56. B
9. B	21. A	33. D	45. B	57. B
10. A	22. C	34. B	46. B	58. B
11. C	23. A	35. C	47. C	59. C
12. A	24. D	36. D	48. A	60. A

1. **The correct answer is B.** Sole proprietorship is the most common form of business ownership in the United States, accounting for almost three quarters of the business organizations in the country. Anyone who runs a business alone is a sole proprietor unless that person has incorporated the business.

2. **The correct answer is A.** Price skimming might seem like a pricing strategy for the decline phase, but it's used at a product introduction in an attempt to recoup costs.

3. **The correct answer is B.** Relocating jobs from the home country to another country because the other country has a lower wage scale involves a question of social responsibility if that means laying off workers and possibly closing a factory or offices in the home country. Doing so would take income away from employees and suppliers of goods and services for both the company and the employees as consumers and deprive municipalities, states, and the federal government of revenue. Price fixing (choice A), harassing a whistleblower (choice C), and reporting inflated profits (choice D) are not matters of social responsibility—they are illegal.

4. The correct answer is B. Building a factory in a foreign country is an example of a direct foreign investment. While there may be some investment in office equipment and supplies, choice A is not the best answer because simply opening an office in a foreign country is not a direct foreign investment. Neither are choices C and D.

5. The correct answer is C. The benefits of a product provide form, time, place, and ownership utility to buyers. Choice A omits ownership. Price, promotion, and place (choice B) are three of the Four P's of marketing; the first is the product itself. Choice D is incorrect because the four types of utility create the value of a product.

6. The correct answer is B. Knowledge information is a type of systems software that allows users to create new types of information. Choices A, C, and D are all systems software that enable managers at different levels in an organization to use data and models to make informed decisions about their departments.

7. The correct answer is A. Corporate philanthropy involves donating some of a company's profits for charitable work, such as sponsoring civic projects like the Great American Cleanup. Refusal to do business with sweatshops (choice B) is an example of CSR related to human rights, not corporate philanthropy. Recycled packaging (choice C) is an example of CSR related to environmental issues. Refusing to allow cigarettes to be used in a program (choice D) is an example of CSR related to marketing and health.

8. The correct answer is D. A major disadvantage of buying an existing business is the possibility of a poor reputation for customer service or poor product quality. The opposite of choice A is true. Buying an existing business takes less time than establishing a new business. The opposite of choice B is true as well; it is easier to get financing for an existing business than a start-up. Choice C is incorrect because the lack of creative control is a disadvantage of buying a new franchise, not an existing business. Once a person owns a nonfranchise business, they can do whatever they believe is necessary for the market.

9. **The correct answer is B.** During a product's growth stage, competitors become aware of the product's surge in sales and market share and begin introducing products to compete with it.

10. **The correct answer is A.** The accounting department is in charge of preparing income statements. Choice C is not the best answer because other departments provide input, which the accounting department then uses to develop budgets. Investing surplus funds (choice B) and determining capitalization strategies (choice D) are functions of financial managers, not accountants.

11. **The correct answer is C.** Encryption software encodes messages so they can't be read without a key, which is "unlocked" with a passphrase. Choice A describes spam-filtering software. Choice B describes anti-spyware software. Choice D describes a firewall.

12. **The correct answer is A.** Selling goods abroad for less than what they cost to produce or less than their domestic price is dumping. While choice B is a practice some manufacturers use, it is not considered dumping. Choice C defines a sale. Choice D is the definition of a subsidy.

13. **The correct answer is C.** Enterprise resource planning program (ERPP) software connects the functions of a business operation. This includes inventory control, scheduling, finance operations, marketing, and human resources.

14. **The correct answer is B.** In a joint venture, both companies will enjoy the benefit of shared resources and information. The downside is the potential for the loss of specialized knowledge and technology and the problems that may arise from sharing control. Choice A is incorrect because in licensing, one company sells the right to its name, product, or process to another and has no control over the resulting business, but it provides a quick entry into a foreign market. A strategic alliance (choice C) is a working arrangement for a period of time and for some specific purpose; neither company cedes its independence or control to the other. In contract manufacturing (choice D), a company contracts with a foreign company to manufacture its product for that foreign market; it provides quick, low-cost entry into the foreign marketplace.

15. **The correct answer is A.** The airline industry, with its few competitors, could be characterized as an oligopoly. An industry that exhibits perfect competition is one with many sellers and buyers, almost no differentiation among products, and low barriers to entry. The airline industry doesn't fit either multiplicity of buyers or low barriers to entry, so choice B is not an accurate characterization. Monopolistic competition describes an industry with many buyers and sellers; buyers believe that there are differences among products, though in reality there aren't. The airline industry doesn't have many sellers, and buyers don't perceive much in the way of differences among those sellers, so choice C is not an accurate characterization either. A monopoly (choice D) has only one seller, and that doesn't describe the airline industry.

16. **The correct answer is B.** Corporate social responsibility involves taking responsibility for the ways in which the company affects the community—internally, domestically, and globally. A company conducting an audit of working conditions in a foreign factory that is producing its smartphone components is an example of exercising corporate social responsibility. Choice A is an example of ethical conduct. Choices C and D are legal issues.

17. **The correct answer is D.** Only capital expenditures such as the construction of new facilities are appropriate reasons for issuing corporate bonds. Research and development (choice A) is paid for normally out of operating expenses (choice B) and issuing corporate bonds to fund operating expenses is not appropriate. Borrowing money to pay interest on borrowed money (choice C) is also not appropriate.

18. **The correct answer is B.** Situation analysis involves looking at internal and external factors that are influencing a business at any given moment. This is a conceptual skill that managers need to be effective. Choice A is an interpersonal ability. Choices C and D are steps in the decision-making process.

19. **The correct answer is D.** The five factors of production are labor, natural resources, capital, entrepreneurs, and technology. Choice A is incorrect because capital is either physical (facilities) or financial (money), and neither technology nor entrepreneurship

fit this definition. Choice B is incorrect because a product mix is the products that a company sells. Choice C is incorrect because operations are the activities that produce a company's goods or services.

20. **The correct answer is A.** A flat structure implies a decentralized organization. A tall structure (choice B) implies a centralized organization (choice C). There is no such thing as an auto-cratic organizational structure (choice D). However, autocratic management would come under the category of an autocratic organization.

21. **The correct answer is A.** A shopping good is one that is bought infrequently and for which a person does research and compar-ison shopping. A computer tablet is an example of a shopping good. A wedding gown (choice B) and an engagement ring (choice D) are classified as specialty goods. A doughnut and coffee (choice C) are typically considered convenience purchases.

22. **The correct answer is C.** The corporate culture is the shared beliefs, values, history, and norms that shape what an organi-zation believes and does. Cross-cultural environments (choice A) are external and affect how businesses operate in countries other than their own. Economic and political-legal environments (choices B and D), are also external influences that affect compa-nies both domestically and internationally.

23. **The correct answer is A.** Net income is gross profit minus oper-ating expenses and income taxes. Choice B is operating income. Choice C is the owner's equity in a business. Choice D is the cost of goods.

24. **The correct answer is D.** Intermediate goals fall typically within the one to five year range. Choices A and B are the time frames for short-term goals. Choice C is not the best answer because a three-year time frame is typically too short for an intermediate goal.

25. **The correct answer is A.** A depreciating currency is declining in value, so imports cost more and exports cost less. Choice B is the opposite of the effect of currency depreciation on imports. Choice C is the opposite of what happens to exports when currency depreciates. Choice D is incorrect because currency depreciation causes imports to rise in price and exports to decline in price.

26. **The correct answer is C.** A Gantt chart shows the steps in a project and the time required to perform the necessary steps. Choice A describes an organization chart. Choice B describes a PERT chart. Choice D is describes a master production schedule.

27. **The correct answer is C.** In relation to the consumer market, the B2B is small. Choices A, B, and D more appropriately characterize the consumer market.

28. **The correct answer is D.** All three factors—ineffective financial controls, lack of adequate capitalization, and inexperienced management—can lead to the failure of a business.

29. **The correct answer is A.** An ISO 9000 label indicates that a company's products adhere to the highest quality. Choice B is similar to the ISO 14000 certification, where a company's products are manufactured in an environmentally friendly way. Choices C and D are not indicators of ISO 9000 certification.

30. **The correct answer is C.** The availability of workers with appropriate skills is an important consideration when determining where to locate a manufacturing facility. Inventory management (choice A) is part of production management and is not related to where to locate a new facility, although it may impact the size of the facility. The size of the market (choice B) is a marketing concern. Choice D is part of laying out a facility, not locating it.

31. **The correct answer is C.** When a country can produce a good more efficiently than other nations, then that country has a comparative advantage in a certain good. Choices A and D both define absolute advantage, not comparative advantage. Choice B is irrelevant.

32. **The correct answer is B.** Arbitration may be binding or not, depending on whether the sides agreed to it being binding or whether they were ordered by a court to binding arbitration. Mediation (choice A) is a recommendation by a third party as to how to end a dispute between parties; it is not a mandatory resolution. Collective bargaining (choice C) is negotiation. A boycott (choice D) is a refusal to buy or use certain products.

33. **The correct answer is D.** Of the choices given, a small business needing money for cash flow would most likely apply for a bank line of credit. It could also apply for a commercial loan, depending on the circumstances. Choice A is incorrect because a debenture is a bond and is a financial tool of large companies, as are choices B and C.

34. **The correct answer is B.** In both e-commerce and traditional sales in the B2B marketplace, there are few customers for any given product. Choice A is incorrect because in both types of selling, orders are generally large. Choice C is incorrect because in both cases, purchasing is centralized in a purchasing department. Choice D is incorrect because comparison shopping to see what competitors offer is routine.

35. **The correct answer is C.** Choice A is the task of the US Treasury Department and is part of fiscal policy, as is choice B. Choice D is the job of the Federal Deposit Insurance Corporation, an independent agency of the federal government.

36. **The correct answer is D.** A balance sheet details a company's assets, liabilities, and owner's equity. Profit and loss (choice A) is shown on an income statement. Choice B is not the best answer because it is not specific. Receipts and payments are shown on a cash flow statement.

37. **The correct answer is C.** The sense of achievement at the end of the project comes from within the employee. Choices A, B, and D are extrinsic motivators.

38. **The correct answer is B.** One of the advantages to taking out a bank loan is that the loan is paid off over a specified length of time, whereas an angel investor is paid a share of the profits for as long as the business exists. While it is true that it is easier for a partnership to get a bank loan, there is no support for the statement in choice A that angel investors prefer to invest in sole proprietorships. If part of an answer is incorrect, the entire answer is incorrect. It is unlikely that a bank will act as an advisor; it is more likely that an angel investor will adopt that role rather than take a hands-of approach, so choice C incorrect. Choice D is irrelevant to a loan status.

39. **The correct answer is A.** Using the internet to recruit a new hire is an external type of recruiting. Choice B is not a recognized term. Posting the job on the company Intranet would be an internal method (choice C). Headhunting (choice D) is employing a company to do one-on-one recruiting for candidates.

40. **The correct answer is B.** Part-time, temporary, and contract workers are contingent workers. While any of the workers listed in choices A, C, and D could be contingent employees depending on the circumstances, a lawyer leased from a company that places lawyers in companies on contract definitely refers to a contingent worker.

41. **The correct answer is C.** A learning organization is a company that changes and adapts to its environment. Choice A may seem like a good choice, but continuous improvement refers to work process engineering. TQM stands for Total Quality Management, which is not the same as adaptability, so choice B is incorrect. Flexible organization (choice D) is not a recognized term.

42. **The correct answer is B.** Statutory law is passed by state legislatures. Choice A describes regulatory law. Choices C and D describe common law.

43. The correct answer is C. The aggregate demand is the amount of goods and services that will be bought at all price levels at a given point in time. The equilibrium point (choice A) is the point at which supply and demand are equal. Aggregate output (choice B) is the total amount of goods and services that an economy produces during a given period of time. The real growth rate (choice D) is the gross domestic product adjusted for inflation and fluctuations in a country's currency.

44. The correct answer is D. All three items are motivators that push people toward becoming entrepreneurs. Three additional reasons are the desire for financial independence, losing one's job, and the desire to capitalize on a great idea.

45. The correct answer is B. Belonging is the third level of Maslow's hierarchy and satisfies the human need for social interaction and acceptance. Safety (choice A) is the second level and refers to feeling safe; while having a safe work environment is part of satisfying this need, the question refers to connectedness, which is more than just feeling safe. Esteem (choice C) is the fourth level and refers to respect, which is more than feeling connected. Self-actualization (choice D) is the highest level and is not dependent on others.

46. The correct answer is B. Malware can be a virus, worm, or Trojan horse. Spyware (choice A) captures information such as passwords, contacts, and credit card numbers and transmits the data back to the sender of the spyware. Spam (choice C) is junk email. Cookies (choice D) are bits of code left in computers when users visit commercial sites that enable the sites to customize pages for viewers.

47. The correct answer is C. Total revenue minus costs of goods sold divided by revenue equals the gross profit margin. Operating expenses (choice A) are the costs of doing business minus income taxes. The operating profit margin (choice B) is total revenue minus cost of goods sold minus operating expenses divided by total revenue. Earnings per share (choice D) is net income divided by number of outstanding shares.

48. **The correct answer is A.** Data mining is analyzing data to find trends and patterns. The question is asking about analyzing data, not interpreting or collecting data as choices B and C indicate. Data drilling (choice D) means "to look at data in increasingly more detailed levels."

49. **The correct answer is C.** The cheap foreign labor argument argues that a protectionist trade policy is needed to combat competition from goods manufactured in developing countries. The bargaining chip argument (choice A) contends that high tariffs can be useful in negotiating with a trading partner to reduce its tariff in exchange for a reduction in comparable tariffs. The infant industry argument (choice B) contends that a developing industry at home needs to be protected from foreign competition. The national security argument (choice D) claims that certain industries should be protected from foreign competition in the interests of their vital importance to the nation's defense.

50. **The correct answer is D.** The right to own property is an essential characteristic of a market economy. Some government control and some competition (choice A) describes an economy with some central planning, also known as socialism. Central planning (choice B) is a characteristic of communist and socialist economies, not market economies. Choice C too narrow; the barrier in any industry may be high or low in a market economy.

51. **The correct answer is A.** Some companies may make junior employees a part of a work team to help them learn their jobs and adjust to the company culture. An apprenticeship (choice B) is a specific type of training program for skilled workers; it would not include information on a company's culture. Mentoring (choice C) is typically found on the managerial level, not on the junior employee level. An orientation program (choice D) describes the company, but not a new employee's job.

52. **The correct answer is D.** Backward scheduling is based on when a product needs to be shipped. Since backward scheduling is used with a variety of inventory systems, policy dictates whether forward or backward scheduling is used, not supplier availability (choice A) or input from a just-in-time inventory control system (choice B). Choice C describes forward scheduling.

53. **The correct answer is C.** Goodwill is a company's intangible asset. Intellectual property (choice A) describes a person's creative output. Liquid assets (choice B) are tangible things that can be easily converted to cash. Choice D is incorrect because brand recognition and a company's reputation are not tangible property.

54. **The correct answer is B.** The promotional mix includes advertising, public relations, sales promotions, and personal selling. The four P's (choice A) are product, price, promotion, and place. The media mix (choice C) is the combination of media used to advertise a product. Product differentiation (choice D) refers to the features of a product that distinguish it from its competitors.

55. **The correct answer is C.** Net income is calculated on total revenue (item I) and operating expenses and income taxes (item III).

56. **The correct answer is B.** The World Bank funds programs to improve conditions and increase productivity in developing nations. Choice A is not a policy of the World Bank. Choice C describes a function of the International Monetary Fund. Choice D is a function of the US Federal Reserve System.

57. **The correct answer is B.** The Federal Fair Labor Standards Act mandates the jobs that must be paid the minimum wage. Choice A is inaccurate; not all jobs are covered by the minimum wage. Choice C is not true because unless violations of the minimum wage are related to job discrimination, the Equal Employment Opportunity Commission would not investigate. Choice D is false; unions use collective bargaining to raise wages whether they are minimum wages or not.

58. **The correct answer is B.** Partnerships find it easier to borrow money because the business doesn't rest on one owner. Choice A is incorrect because neither sole proprietorships nor partnerships enjoy limited liability. Choice C is incorrect because partnerships require more paperwork to establish than do sole proprietorships. Choice D is incorrect because sole proprietorships and partnerships have similar tax benefits; in both, owners pay taxes as personal income.

59. **The correct answer is C.** Like catalog shopping, consumers can't see and touch the products they are interested in buying. The opposite of choices A and B is true. Comparison shopping is easier and the product array is larger than a consumer would have in local stores. Choice D is inaccurate because prices are comparable or even lower than in brick-and-mortar stores.

60. **The correct answer is A.** Like bounce-back coupons and discount coupons, point-of-sale displays are sales promotion strategies. Advertising (choice B) is not a sales promotion technique; product placement in a movie or TV show is an example of advertising a product. A distribution channel (choice C) is a way to move goods from producer to consumer. While a point-of-sale display may prompt an impulse buy, choice D is incorrect because this is a sales promotion technique.

Like what you see? Get unlimited access to Peterson's full catalog of DSST practice tests, instructional videos, flashcards, and more at **www.petersons.com/testprep/dsst**.